Ab

Lisa Webb has been writing as a Canadian Expat Mom for many years, across many continents. She's the author of the series *The Kids Who Travel the World* and the editor and publisher of the anthologies *Once Upon an Expat* and *Life on the Move*, which have been a platform for brave and courageous women to share their stories of living abroad. Lisa is using her experience as a global citizen to connect to women across Canada and beyond, through her heart-centred company, Wine, Women & Well-Being.

BECOMING FRENCH

Lisa Webb

BECOMING FRENCH

Vanguard Press

VANGUARD PAPERBACK

© Copyright 2021
Lisa Webb

The right of Lisa Webb to be identified as author of
this work has been asserted by her in accordance with the
Copyright, Designs and Patents Act 1988.

All Rights Reserved

No reproduction, copy or transmission of this publication
may be made without written permission.
No paragraph of this publication may be reproduced,
copied or transmitted save with the written permission of the
publisher, or in accordance with the provisions
of the Copyright Act 1956 (as amended).

Any person who commits any unauthorised act in relation to
this publication may be liable to criminal
prosecution and civil claims for damages.

A CIP catalogue record for this title is
available from the British Library.

ISBN 978 1 784656 62 1

*Vanguard Press is an imprint of
Pegasus Elliot MacKenzie Publishers Ltd.*
www.pegasuspublishers.com
First Published in 2021

**Vanguard Press
Sheraton House Castle Park
Cambridge England**

Printed & Bound in Great Britain

Dedication

For my daughters, Océane and Elodie.

May you always have the bravery to chase new adventures, and the courage to follow your hearts.

Prelude

What was I thinking?

I had a great career. I had job security. I had a pension. My parents were so proud. "Our daughter, a school administrator in the big city, and at such a young age!"

So, what did I do? I quit. Just like that.

Now, I didn't flip over my desk and throw piles of paper into the air or anything. But I did clear out my office, said goodbye to my colleagues, and against every rational brain cell I had, I willingly became unemployed.

I had only been married for a few months; the vows were still fresh in my mind. They were the standard vows, said at most weddings, but if I had to rewrite them, it might sound something like this.

I Lisa, take you Kevin, to be my husband.
I will quit my job for you.
Follow you to a foreign land where I don't speak the language.
I will spend my days unemployed, without any family or friends.

And when it all gets to be too much, I will cry into a baguette and a glass of Bordeaux.

For as long as we both shall live, so help me God.

A bit dramatic? Maybe. But we were moving to Paris and it was the craziest thing I'd ever done.

My husband would be working, and speaking French without issue because he was perfectly bilingual. While I'd be… well, that was yet to be decided.

Life as I Knew It

Tears were rolling down my cheeks and my mascara was following close behind. I had just finished my second glass of wine, but I would have been crying even if I hadn't been drinking. I couldn't hold myself together any longer, and as I tilted my head back to try and stop the tears, the table beside us looked over. My girlfriends exchanged a concerned glance.

"Whatever it is, we'll figure it out."

My childhood best friend and I had moved to the same city after university. I could always count on her to have my back.

I took the cloth napkin off my lap and used it to compose myself. "Kev got a job offer. I think we have to move to Paris."

I slumped in my chair, completely miserable as my three best friends, out for our monthly dinner, let out an unanimous groan.

"Paris?" Monika piped up first, with her natural gift for lightening heavy situations. Her quick wit was one of the things I loved most about her. "Paris is your big problem? I *wish* I had Paris-problems!" And with that she topped up everybody's wine, then eyed the server for another bottle. We were going to be there awhile.

Our monthly girls' dinners had started seven years earlier when we all met in our adoptive city to start our careers, and it had become a monthly ritual ever since. We knew by now that whenever a dinner involved one of us crying we'd be shutting down the restaurant.

"Lis, I kinda agree with Monika," Jackie said gently, always thinking before she spoke. "That doesn't seem like such a bad problem to have."

"Okay, pros and cons." Karen interjected, now in full psychologist mode even though I was far from a paying client. "Why don't you walk us through the details?"

Having a moment to gather myself, I felt better prepared to tell the full story.

"You guys know how much I love my job. In seven years of teaching the only time I've ever disliked going to work in the morning was when we used to have these dinners on a Thursday night and I'd have a massive wine headache on Friday morning." Understanding nods came from around the table. "And now that I've finally finished my master's degree and got the promotion to Assistant Principal, I love work even more. I feel like the situation isn't really balanced. Kev gets to keep his job, actually, he now gets a promotion, plus he already speaks perfect French, so that's not an issue. And his family doesn't live here, so moving away doesn't change how often he'll see them."

There were more understanding nods, but they knew I wasn't finished and waited for me to get it all out. I took a sip of wine and continued.

"I'll have to quit my job; I don't speak French..."

"Remember how you told Kevin you did on your first date when he said it was his first language," Monika couldn't help but add to lighten the mood. "I digress. Keep going."

"As I was saying," I raised my eyebrows playfully in Monika's direction, "besides having no job and not speaking the language, I also won't have any family there. My brothers both just had kids, and you know I love our Sunday family dinners. Kev and I have only been married a couple of months. We're still getting used to being an 'us' instead of an 'I' and now all these life changing decisions need to be made. I know marriage is a compromise, but this just feels like a really lopsided one." I exhaled, leaning back into my chair, feeling better already for having got that out.

Karen always knew how to make me laugh. "I bet they didn't mention any of this in that marriage class you guys had to take before your wedding."

"Not even close."

"Well, do you *have* to go?" Jackie asked.

"No, we don't *have* to. Of course Kevin said the decision was ours to make together, and if I really didn't want to, we could stay. But it's such a great opportunity for his career, and I know he really wants to take it, so I want to support him. It just feels really hard to do right now. And that's just the emotional side of the decision. The logistics are a nightmare. Do we sell the house we just bought, or rent it? What do we do with all of our stuff? There's no way it'll fit into a Parisian apartment. Kev and I are both so independent that we don't even have a joint bank account. Now I'm going to have no job? What will I do for money? Ask him for an allowance if I want to buy something? That might kill me!"

All the unknowns made this whole thing feel like a crazy leap of faith.

Our girls' night didn't end with me having all the answers, or even feeling more confident in my decision. But as always, it felt so good to be able to talk it out with my girlfriends. Just add that to the list of things that I was going to miss about the life I was about to leave behind.

This move was going to bring a different dynamic to our relationship. In that moment we had so many different people in our lives: friends, colleagues, sibling, parents and of course each other. In Paris it would be just the two of us. If we took this chance and made it though, it would surely make us stronger.

During those decision-making days, there were debates, tears, and moments of slight insanity on my part. I was so unsure. Yet, when the day came to give an official answer and sign on the dotted line, as uneasy as I was, our answer was yes. The offer was too good to pass up and my gut knew it. Whether I was ready or not, we were moving to Paris.

We were about to embark on the experience of a lifetime.

Sight Unseen

Stability was something I took for granted until it was lifted out of my life. I suddenly felt like a tree being ripped out of the ground, roots exposed and in shock, with only a vague plan of being planted back in a completely different environment, say between two pieces of cobblestone, and hoping it would flourish.

Flourishing did not happen right away. There were a lot of things that did happen between the time we decided Kevin would take the offer, and the moment we arrived in Paris, but flourishing was definitely not one of them.

I'd heard that the first year of marriage was the hardest. I had to agree. We just emptied the entire contents of our new home, save for what we could fit in a couple of suitcases. We were treading lightly as we both tried to refrain from making the other justify what got to come with us and what didn't make the cut. By the time the house was empty I was genuinely surprised that I couldn't taste blood in my mouth from biting my tongue all day. Kevin and I were taking our first steps on the tightrope of matrimony and were trying to keep our balance while carrying those suitcases across an ocean. The globe was spinning around me and my new unrecognisable life was making me dizzy.

I put on the bravest face I could muster, clutching Kevin's arm with my right hand, and pulling a carry-on, full of anxiety, with my left. I was determined to see this as an adventure, even if I couldn't imagine how it would all play out.

"This is it!" I said hesitantly to my still-new husband as the plane screeched to a halt on the tarmac at Charles de Gaulle Airport.

It was our new beginning and my greatest act of love to date. I was putting someone else's feelings and intentions above my own. At thirty-years-old I was finally in 'grown up' love. For better or worse. And I couldn't help feeling like our better and worse was about to happen at the exact same time.

"There he is." Kevin pointed as he spotted the driver sent by his company. He was holding a sign with our last name. We walked toward it, ready to begin our new life.

"Kehvin et Leeza?"

"Oui, c'est nous." Kevin confirmed our identity, but I wasn't sure why because I didn't recognise either of the names the man had said.

After a few brief pleasantries with our driver, none of which I understood, we were on our way. He continued to call me Leeza, instead of Lisa, but I didn't really mind. Maybe that would be my French name, like an alter-ego.

I was anxious beyond belief to find out where we were going to live. As if moving to a foreign country isn't a big enough adventure, we were also about to be dropped off at the apartment we would be living in for the next year. We hadn't seen any pictures or gotten a single detail.

It had been arranged through the company Kevin worked for that after being picked up at the airport, we would be dropped outside our building, and met by a woman who would give us the keys to our apartment. Meaning, wherever this man dropped us off was going to be where we would live. No options, or asking to see a few more places. That would be it. Sight unseen.

This game of roulette had me critically assessing every building we passed and my over active imagination conjuring up all sorts of scenarios in my mind.

"Imagine if he dropped us off on the Champs-Élysées. A penthouse with a view of the Arc de Triomphe," I whispered to Kevin, beside me in the back of the car.

One of us had to be a realist, and that was Kevin's role in our relationship. "Love, unless you want to be really disappointed, maybe set the bar a little lower on your day-dreaming."

He had a point. But with one extreme came another and I was back to whispering my thoughts out loud. "What if he drops us off at some rat-infested hell hole with no hot water. And a crazy cat lady next door that shouts things in French when we walk by."

"Maybe it's best if we just wait until we get there." He smiled, taking my hand to calm my nerves.

When the driver finally dropped us off in front of our building, I breathed a sigh of relief. It seemed okay. I looked up at a newer building, in what seemed like a nice neighbourhood, and thus far, I was the only crazy lady in sight.

Waiting for the relocation agent to bring the keys felt like an eternity, but in reality it was probably about twenty minutes. Twenty long minutes, and an innumerable amount of irrational thoughts spinning through my mind.

What if he dropped us off at the wrong place and this lady doesn't show up? I wonder if the beds are comfy? What if they suck? We'll end up with bad backs. Maybe this is the lady? Or this car pulling up? I wonder if it's big inside? Or maybe it's incredibly small? Will there be a closet? Maybe she forgot about us.

When the woman finally did arrive, it was such a relief to stop my busy mind, that I no longer cared what the place looked like. I just wanted the uncertainty to be over. This was what we'd been waiting for. Our moment of truth had arrived!

Full of suspense, we followed her into the building like two overly anxious little ducklings trailing behind her, unable to contain our curiosity of what the future would hold.

"So far so good, right?" Kevin confirmed with me as we walked into the foyer nervously. "There's even an elevator."

I was also pleasantly surprised by that. It wasn't a given in Paris.

"It's new too!" I was happy with how modern it was. When I travelled to Paris nearly a decade earlier, I remember being in tiny elevators that would barely fit my backpack, and there was a metal gate that had to be pulled across the door manually before the elevator would start. The elevator in our new building was just like any regular elevator I'd see back home. It even had enough room for the three of us, plus an automatically closing door. Things were looking up!

As the realtor put the key in the slot of our apartment door, we were both peering over her shoulder, afraid of what might be hiding behind on the other side.

She flung open the door and the sound of us both exhaling in relief was probably heard by the neighbours, who turned out to be a nice normal family, with no cats.

Our apartment wasn't the penthouse suite, but it also wasn't a rat-infested hell hole. It had original hardwood floors and a nice big living room with a pull-out couch for guests. We had two bedrooms, which was more than enough space for just the two of us, and a bathroom with a tub/shower combo. Of course, no French apartment would be complete without a WC (water closet), or as I liked to call it, the tiny little room with the toilet where my elbows could touch both walls. Although a modern building, we weren't spared a few little Parisian quirks, like having our washer under the bathroom sink and our dryer in the kitchen. I was happy the dryer was there though, because the top of it made up fifty percent of the counter space in our tiny *cuisine*.

We'd soon come to know the lay of the land. You don't dare get in or out of the elevator without a *Bonjour* or a *Bonsoir* to your fellow neighbour; the French are serious about their formal pleasantries. We knew from looking out our balcony that the lady in the apartment across the street was a chain smoker who spent most of her days on her adjacent balcony, puffing away. And the smell coming from the *Boulangerie* below us was enough to make me gain five pounds just from breathing.

With the giant, old-fashioned keys to our apartment finally in our possession, we both flopped ourselves back on the couch. We made it. We now had our very own Parisian apartment and we liked the place. It wasn't huge, but it had everything we needed. Things were going to be okay.

Until they weren't.

Finding My Way

We spent the first week exploring our new city. There's no denying that Paris is magical. Every corner was a hidden gem, every street impressive. We picnicked, ate, drank and dined. It was the ultimate vacation until reality brought it all to a screeching halt.

Kevin had to go to work on Monday, out of town.

We'd been in our new city for less than a week and he had to leave. I didn't want to be a baby about being left alone so soon. So instead I chose to be the strong independent woman he married. I held my head high as I wished him *bon voyage*.

"I'll be back on Sunday," he told me. "And with any luck our stuff might arrive while I'm gone."

In the meantime, I sat in our mostly empty apartment, wondering where to begin. I lived in Paris now, which was surreal. But, I was unemployed, illiterate, and I didn't know a soul. I had no idea what to do with myself. We had already spent a week exploring, and I could only be a 'tourist' for so long. With Kevin at work, the newness of our arrival had lost its novelty, leaving me alone, with an urgent need to create some kind of a life for myself in my new city.

Instead of staying home and crying about not having any friends, which I briefly debated, I decided instead, I would take myself out for dinner that night.

While I used the giant decorative-looking key to lock the door, I was very aware that this would be the first time I'd ever gone to a restaurant alone. An extrovert never eats alone when they have a long list of people to call and join them when they feel like grabbing a bite to eat. But here in Paris, I was alone, and quickly realised this whole experience was going to happen in French. I suddenly never felt more introverted in my life.

Kevin insisted on me taking French lessons before we moved to help ease my transition. But having spent all my time with him until now, it was clear that I had been relying heavily on his French skills and completely neglecting mine. Without my husband's flawless French to hide behind, I was forced to open my mouth and give it a shot. I pushed down my apprehension and asked for a table, "*Une table pour un s'il vous plait.*"

Alone in a romantic restaurant, without even a phone to keep me company, because just like my confidence in dining alone, my phone didn't exist yet either. I ordered a glass of wine and tried to be the strong woman I used to be, just a few short weeks ago. I summoned her to keep me company, because that chair across the table for two never felt so huge and empty. I was sure that the topic of conversation at everyone else's table in the restaurant was the lone foreign girl eating by herself.

This was not me. I was not the kind of person who had self-destructive thoughts; if anything I was over-confident in most aspects of my life, perhaps to a fault. But there I was, one person, at a table for two, unable to stop the cycle of toxic self-commentary about how I'd royally screwed up my life. I couldn't help going back to the fact that I'd worked so hard to get where I was before we moved. What was I thinking? The idea of starting from scratch in a country where I couldn't read, write or speak, seemed too huge to tackle. And right there in that restaurant, with the neighbouring table uncomfortably close, my courage abandoned me, and I hit my breaking point.

"*Vous êtes prêtes, madame?*" The stuffy waiter asked if I was ready to order with an undertone of annoyance in his voice.

I looked down at the menu, unable to read more than a couple of words, and feeling completely overwhelmed with my unravelled life. I started sobbing into my glass of Bordeaux.

"*Je vais vous donner une minute.*" He offered to give me a minute and disappeared.

That dinner was a long, painful one, and unfortunately, not the last of its kind. But I slowly took that sad girl in the restaurant and tried to get her back on track. By no means was it an easy task. I felt like an unconfident, awkward teenager, unsure of where I fit in the world, or where my life was going.

Taking up permanent residence in Paris was a different experience from when I had visited as a tourist. The charm of the city of lights fade ever so slightly when it comes to the matter of getting on with everyday life.

***

'I'm going to go get some groceries. Let me know if you need anything.' I texted Kevin at work the following week so he wouldn't be worried that I was at home drowning my sorrows in a tub of ice cream.

Not having a car meant I had to walk to get groceries, another first for me. I put on some comfortable shoes and made my way down the street towards the grocery store.

Before moving to Paris I bought my groceries at big box stores where I'd indulge my inner hoarder by filling the cart with enough food to fill our fridge, overflow into our spare fridge, and then I'd put all the frozen items in the deep freeze. Kevin is a very large man, in the 'I'm going to eat several chicken breasts and then go do some exercise' kind of way, not to be confused with the 'he eats too many potato chips' look. I had gotten used to feeding him and the amount of groceries that took.

Obviously things needed to change if I was carrying my groceries home. But this was a lesson I'd yet to learn.

"Kev, are you almost done at work? I need help!" I panted into the cell phone that was pinned between my shoulder and ear. I was out of breath and I'd barely made it half a block.

"What's wrong? Did something happen?" He was sounding concerned. Which made sense since I needed him now in so many more ways than I had before. Overnight his wife had gone from self-sufficient-career-woman, to a slightly depressed foreigner that didn't speak the language. He worried about me. It was sweet and, from my recent track record, not completely unnecessary.

"I bought too many groceries and I thought I would be able to make it home, but now my hands feel like they're going to start bleeding from carrying the heavy bags. I'm pretty sure I've given myself tennis elbow or something. I can't make it home."

I heard an exhale that was a combination of relief and exasperation. "Seriously, Lis? You want me to leave work to come and help you carry the groceries home?"

"Well, no…" I was sounding and feeling a little sheepish now, "I guess not. I just put too much in the cart, and then at the checkout when I remembered I had to carry it all home I didn't want to hold up the line and I couldn't explain the problem in French to the lady at the check-out who wouldn't dare crack a smile. So I just bought everything, thinking I might be able to carry it but now it's too much and this is the first time I've spoken to anyone all day because no one in the country speaks English!"

By now I was looking and sounding a bit neurotic, standing in the street, forbidding myself to cry, surrounded by enough groceries to sustain a French family of five for several weeks.

I apologised to Kevin for calling him at work with such a trivial problem. Really, I was just lonely and overwhelmed, needing a friendly voice in that moment. I eventually got home on my own, cursing myself for going to the grocery store hungry.

Kevin came home from work that night pulling one of those wheeled carts that elderly ladies use for their groceries. "I love you.' He offered it to me with a smile. "We'll get there, Lis. We're still finding our way here."

I didn't know whether to laugh, or my new go-to emotion, cry. At home these grocery carts were for little old grannies, but I had to admit that I saw a bunch of people with them at the grocery store. I accepted the gift with gratitude and gave my husband a giant hug, allowing all the frustration of the day to melt away. As long as we were together, we'd be okay.

Side Tracked

To avoid staying at home and focusing on the fact that I didn't have a job to go to, each day I would give myself a little project to keep busy. Sometimes I'd pick a different neighbourhood to explore, other days I'd go out in search of things we needed for the house, which always ended up taking far longer than expected.

When we moved, we left appliances that needed to be plugged in back home because the electrical sockets wouldn't be compatible. That left us with a lot of household items to replace, and I decided it had been long enough since I'd properly dried my hair. The job of the day was going to be buying a new hair dryer.

Roaming the aisles of the store didn't lead me to what I was looking for. At home there would have been an entire section of hair dryers and curling irons, making it hard to miss. I reminded myself, once again, that I was a long way from home. I turned the corner to the next aisle and seeing someone stocking the shelves, I let out a little sigh of relief that this employee would be able to help me. Following my natural instinct, I walked right over to ask where I could find what I was looking for. But when I arrived in front of the young man, he turned to look at me, and I remembered that I didn't actually know how to verbalise what I needed. I stood frozen for a second as I searched for the right words.

"Bonjour, madame," he greeted me, his face questioning what I wanted.

Cheveux was the French word for hair. Growing up in Canada with all products having English on one side and French on the other, meant that years of staring at the back side of shampoo bottles while taking extra-long showers as a teenager taught me that hair in French was indeed *cheveux*. But it hadn't taught me much more than that. 'Hair-dryer' was not in my vocabulary, nor was how to string together a sentence good enough to explain that I was looking to buy one.

I quickly thought of my French lessons: '*Je cherche*' meant, 'I am looking'. It wasn't a full sentence, but it was a start and as far as I was going to get in that moment. The shelf stocker was staring at me on the verge of impatience, so I had to just give it my best shot.

"*Je cherche…*" but I didn't know the word for hair dryer, only hair, leaving me no other choice but to show him. I tried to make my hand into something that resembled a hairdryer, pointed it toward my head, and then made the corresponding hair dryer sound with my mouth.

I was met with a blank stare. Not knowing what to do next, I delved deeper into the charades, holding up my hair with my left hand, and flipping it around with the imaginary hair dryer that was my right hand, then offering, "*cheveux*".

Now he was looking slightly concerned. Come to think of it, the make-shift hair dryer I had made with my hand was the same way young kids fashioned imaginary guns. He could really be getting the wrong message. I was starting to sweat from the stress. I'd give it one more try.

"Je cherche cheveux drier," I offered, continuing the charades for lack of any other bright ideas.

There was a long pause before he opened his mouth. "A hair dryer?" He responded in almost perfect English.

Are you kidding me! He spoke English and let me go on totally embarrassing myself for far longer than necessary.

"Yes, a hair dryer," I confirmed, red-faced.

I grabbed the first one I saw, said, "*merci*", paid, and bolted out the door. If nothing else, living in Paris was keeping me humble.

I walked home, trying to shake off the humiliation of my one-sided charades game, sauntering along at the pace of someone with nowhere particularly important to be.

"*Excusez-moi, mademoiselle!*" called out a small elderly woman standing in front of an apartment building. Being married meant that I was technically a 'madame' and 'mademoiselle' was reserved for younger, unmarried girls. But relatively speaking, I was a young girl compared to this woman who had to be in her eighties.

I spun around seeing if it was actually me she was talking to, and confirmed by pointing at myself, "Me?"

"*Oui, oui, pouvez-vous m'aider?*" She motioned for me to come over.

I didn't understand what she said, but once I got a little closer she continued talking and reached out to grab my arm.

"*Désolé je ne parle pas français.*" One phrase I had mastered was telling people that I couldn't speak French.

She continued talking to me anyway in the rapid speed of someone who was most definitely Parisienne. Taking my arm, she motioned for me to cross the street. I didn't know what she was actually saying to me, but I was getting to be quite good at guessing. I could tell she had trouble walking and needed help with her balance. Her smile was heartwarming, and I couldn't help but think of my own grandmothers back home, in their eighties as well. With both of her arms hanging on tightly to mine, we crossed the road as one.

I looked at her, wondering what would happen next, and she pointed up the street towards a 'Tabac' stand that sold newspapers and cigarettes. She said something else in French that I didn't understand and made no move towards letting go of my arm. Then she started taking a step forward, so I joined her, letting her use my arm to keep her balance.

As she walked up the road she continued to chatter away in French, and not picking up a single word she said, I offered her what little French I had at the pace of a toddler speaking their first words.

"*Je m'appelle Lisa. Je parle anglais. Je suis nouveau ici.*" In very basic sentences, I told her my name, that I spoke English, and that I was new to Paris. She had probably figured everything except my name out on her own already, but I was trying, and frankly, even though we couldn't communicate, we seemed to be equally enjoying each other's company. Maybe like me, she was a bit lonely during the days, and perhaps she had a grand-daughter that I reminded her of, just like she had me thinking of, and missing, my grandmas.

When we finally got to the *tabac,* the man working there seemed to know her and greeted her kindly, then looked and me and gave me the same warm smile he gave her. He said something in French to me, to which I smiled and nodded, then I took the newspaper that my temporary grandmother passed me and tucked it under my arm.

Looking at her once again for guidance, she motioned that she wanted to cross the adjacent street and this time I picked up the word, "*boulangerie*". She wanted to go to the bakery that was just on the other side of the road. So off we went, moving along at a snail's pace.

I couldn't help but wonder how long this little side-outing was going to go on for. I was also getting more frustrated by the day that becoming fluent in French wasn't coming as quickly or easily as I'd hoped. It would have made strange situations like this much easier.

After helping my new friend buy her bread, I was now carrying her newspaper *and* her baguette under my left arm as she held onto my right, not loosening her grip for a moment since I had met her nearly half an hour earlier, except for handing out her carefully counted centimes to pay for the items.

Thankful that I didn't have anywhere to be, I wondered how she normally got around. We slowly walked back to where we initially met, and I decoded that she actually lived in the building she was standing in front of when she stopped me. She had me help her up the two stairs to the door, passed me her keys to open the front door and once helping her into the main area of the building, the apartment 'guardien' took over from there. They both thanked me and wished me "*bon journée*".

Having felt like I saturated my language barrier quota of the day, I made a beeline for my apartment, eyes down, not feeling strong enough to endure another game of foreigner charades.

Kevin came home to me watching dubbed over 90210 in hopes of picking up some French vocabulary.

"What does *couché* mean?" I asked as he hung up his keys.

"To sleep. Why?"

"Ahh, that makes sense. I'm watching 90210 in French and someone is always 'couché'ing' with someone else's boyfriend."

He laughed. "Whatever it takes to get you practising your French."

I got off the couch and went to meet him by the kitchen. "When I tell you about the day I had, I think you'll agree, I need a lot more than 90210 to help me with my French."

"So I'll open some wine then?" he suggested, already knowing the answer.

"Now there's something I love about this country." And I passed him the corkscrew.

Speed Dating

Just around the corner from our neighbourhood grocery store was where I went for French classes. I'd often leave class and head directly to buy food for dinner because I'd be so hungry from all the food-talk in class. And because I was now trying to shop in smaller quantities.

"Qu'est-ce que vous mangez pour diner ce soir?" My teacher, Karine, asked. Like many people in France, she loved to talk about food. It seemed like every time I had a class she wanted to know what I was having for dinner.

"Je ne sais pas encore." I told her I didn't know yet and we proceeded to discuss my options *en francais,* of course.

Our classes often went this way. Initially, I started taking big group classes but found that my lazy gene would kick in, and it was far too easy to let someone with a better command of the language answer the questions and do all the talking. Determined to get to a level where I could at least function in French society without being completely embarrassed, I switched to one-on-one classes several times per week and that's when I landed in Karine's class.

We were both foodies in our own way. She liked to cook and I liked to eat... mostly at restaurants because I hadn't honed in on my culinary skills yet.

As I packed up my books I attempted small talk by telling her I was going to the grocery store, literally pointing in the direction of the store to clarify my point.

"*Puis-je vous rejoindre?*" she asked, eagerly with a smile but I had no idea what she said.

I smiled back but there must have been a blank stare on my face because she repeated herself, now also pointing in the same direction of the grocery store.

"*Puis-je vous rejoindre a Monoprix?*"

Monoprix. That was the name of the grocery store. She wanted to come with me to the store.

"*Ahhhhh, toi et moi?*" You and me? I asked for clarification.

She smiled and nodded while I panicked inside. Obviously I couldn't say no. That would be far too rude, but this was going to be so awkward. I had the French communication skills of a toddler, which was fine inside the walls of the classroom, but now she wanted to come to the grocery store with me. I could barely speak to her.

Without the vocabulary to get any further into this conversation, I smiled, nodded and off we went in awkward silence.

As time went on, if Karine didn't have another student after me, which she often didn't since it was late in the day, she would join me on my trips to the grocery store. I was slowly learning that she truly was a product of her culture, being genuinely passionate about food. During our French class we'd practise my vocabulary by discussing a recipe, the required ingredients, and the how-to's of the instructions. Then after class, we'd either make a trip to the grocery store, or straight to my apartment, where she'd teach me how to cook simple French dishes.

We started with crepes. It was really basic, but I wasn't exactly Martha Stewart in the kitchen, so we needed to start out slowly. The measurements were all different from what I was accustomed to, so that took some getting used to. French recipes don't use cups and teaspoons, instead ingredients are measured by weight.

"La prochaine fois nous allons vous acheter une balance alimentaire." She told me that next time we had to buy a food scale. But I wasn't positive that's what she said because I usually only picked up half of our conversations. Generally, when she realised I didn't understand, she would revert to charades for my benefit.

She showed me the ropes in my new French kitchen, not at all flustered by the fact that we were prepping ingredients on the top of my dryer. It wasn't long before she had me whipping up molten lava cakes for Kevin and I, or as she called them *fondant au chocolat*.

Karine was great, but the relationship was difficult for me.

Kevin was the only French speaker that I really knew, but he was perfectly bilingual, and since we met in English, that was our common language. Even when we tried to practise French together so I could improve, I would get frustrated, and switch back to English within minutes. So when I met Karine, it was nice that she was not only my French teacher, but becoming a friend. I was also the first English-speaking friend she'd ever made, which makes sense because she didn't actually speak any English, or at least not that I'd heard.

"I think I might need to break up with Karine," I said to Kevin over dinner one night.

"Why? She's good for you. Your French is really improving." He was being kind. 'Improving' meant that it was no longer non-existent. I was far from impressing anyone with my language skills.

"She just took me on an eight-hour French date. I couldn't escape! My head feels like it's going to explode!"

As we left the apartment and walked toward the nearest Metro station, I filled Kevin in on how we'd gone to her apartment so she could teach me to make macarons, which was amazing, but those little things take forever to make. I was there nearly all day. Then we went to a tea house and after that she wanted to go shopping. It sounds like a great day, until you think about doing all that in a language you're just learning. It was the most mentally exhausting thing I'd ever done.

"I actually fell asleep when I got home. It was like my brain ran a marathon… in stiletto heels!"

Kevin laughed and ushered me into the Metro ahead of him. "A glass of wine will fix you right up." He smiled.

"That seems to be my new trend in this country."

I never broke up with Karine, even though there were days I wanted to. She felt like one of those boyfriends that your mom liked more than you did: Mr Right, at the wrong time.

My French was improving, Kevin was right about that. My new friendship *was* good for me, and I now had my first real French friend. I just had to take it easy on the power dates in order to save my sanity.

As great as Karine was, and as much as I knew it was important to immerse myself in the French way of life, I couldn't help by miss having English-speaking girlfriends. Karine was good for my French, but an English-speaking friend would be good for my soul. I missed my girlfriends back home and our nights out where we'd stay late at restaurants drinking wine and talking louder by the glass. I never appreciated the simple act of being able to talk, until I couldn't do it any more.

Finding my tribe in Paris was harder than I thought. I'd always made friends rather easily, but Paris was a cheeky little bugger. Everyone I met was either transient, on the next plane out, or in a different stage of their life, so we didn't quite click.

"Maybe they're all hiding in some great bar that I don't know about," I joked to Kevin.

"I've got to give you credit for trying. If they were hiding in markets, malls, libraries or parks, you'd have found them by now. You've been looking!" He paused, then added, "You even went speed dating."

I swatted him. "It wasn't speed dating!"

"Oh no? What was it then?" he joked.

"It was an attempt to find some girlfriends and improve my French at the same time," I said, matter-of-factly. Then upon further reflection added, "Well, maybe it was a bit like speed dating but I was only looking for girlfriends."

My Parisian speed dating experience was unique if nothing else. For ten euros I got entrance to the event and a glass of wine. As soon as I went in I scanned the room for any potential friends. Stifling away my disappointment that no one ran over and declared me their new BFF, I chalked it up as an opportunity to practise my French and took a seat on the 'English' side of the table. Soon after, all the French people took a seat on the other side. We spoke in English for ten minutes, then a bell chimed and we had to talk in French for another ten minutes. It sounds easy, but speaking French with a complete stranger for ten minutes straight with my limited vocabulary was painful, for both sides of the table. Until the second half of the night where I'd get to refill my wine glass. On my second glass of wine, my inhibitions fell and I didn't really care about the mistakes I was making, giving myself the freedom to make errors without feeling overly embarrassed. Two glasses and up was where my best French came out.

It was at that language exchange that I learned I wasn't quite as Parisienne as I was hoping. I was chatting with a very nice, born and raised, Parisian, who in hindsight was not trying to be a jerk, but was just bluntly pointing out the obvious, as the French often do.

"You're from America," he said as he greeted me and sat down across the table.

When I clarified that I was actually Canadian, I asked how he knew I wasn't from the UK or another English-speaking country. He replied, "You're all dressed up like ze Christmas tree," and he nodded his head toward the brightly decorated tree in the corner of the room.

I paused a moment to take in what he was trying to tell me. He went on to say that us 'North American' woman dress ourselves up like decorated Christmas trees: highlight our hair, wear lots of makeup and jewellery, just like you would do to an *arbre de Noel*.

I had a quick review of myself: my highlights and curled hair were my tinsel, dangly earrings, necklace, bracelet, rings, could easily be seen as my decorations and I had a face full of makeup with my lips as red as Christmas holly.

"*Touché, monsieur.*"

I glanced over at the French side of the tables. The women were all well put together but in a very understated way. They all let their hair do what it did naturally: generally not coloured, curled or straightened. If it was curly, they wore it curly, and straight hair stayed straight. If they were wearing makeup, it was very natural, and their shoes were flat, probably with feet inside that were not covered in blisters like mine, because Parisiennes know that they'll be walking a lot, so they wear stylish, yet practical and versatile shoes. There's no fashion in limping from a twisted ankle on cobblestone.

As my sore feet carried me home that night, I realised that the blunt Frenchman was onto something. Functional fashion was where it's at.

My quest for female friendship often ended with me hobbling home on cobblestone in my too high of heels and sore feet, making a mental note to change my footwear in accordance to these old European streets. If I happened to find somewhere open, I'd pop in and grab some chocolates or a little bag of caramel beurre sale macarons, swearing I'd save them for throughout the week, but almost always end up with a crumpled-up empty bag by the time I walked through the front door.

That 'speed dating' night I walked back into our apartment slightly deflated. One look at me and Kevin opened his arms, ready for the hug, knowing I'd struck out yet again before he even asked.

"Don't be discouraged, Lis." He pulled me in, getting me settled beside him on the couch. "Let's watch some horrible French TV."

"Sure. Nothing makes me feel better like watching a television program dubbed over in French so the lips don't match the words."

"I see your sense of humour is still in check." He grinned.

Croissant-Top

About a year before we moved to Paris, I took up running. I'd done a few races and when we landed in France I was midway through a half-marathon training program. I loved using it as a way to explore the city, and I finally managed to meet some English-speaking girls through a running group I found online. There were a couple of problems with this running group though. First, I hate talking while I run, making it difficult to ask or answer questions, so although I wasn't shy, it sure seemed that way. Second, these runners were mostly new moms, which meant that they were up at the crack of dawn every Saturday morning no matter what. When you have kids that wake up before the sun, you're totally ready to meet with a running group by nine a.m.

I, however, did not have kids, and meeting these girls at nine a.m. required me to leave my apartment at eight thirty on Saturday mornings. As everybody knows, Saturday morning follows Friday night, which usually meant that Kevin and I were out exploring the city the night before, eating and drinking just a little more than necessary. I had no children, placing me in the 'sleep until ten a.m.' stage of my life. Needless to say, as good as my intentions were, I didn't make it to the running group as often as I would have if it were one p.m. on Saturday afternoon.

My mom and aunts were in Paris visiting, and we were about to take a little side trip to Italy, so my attempt to join the early morning running group would be put on hold for what I thought would be a few weeks. Turns out it was going to be far more than that.

***

We were making our way to Tuscany by train, with tickets from Milan to Lucca, with a brief stop to change trains in Bologna. As I was the token traveller in the group, my mom and aunts put me in charge. I had all the train tickets and the villa information in my purse. When the ladies questioned which stop we got off on, I told them, "Our final stop won't be on this screen, just remember we have to switch trains in Bologna. It sounds like Boloney, so we won't forget."

I started to feel antsy and it wasn't long before I was bored. As the train slowed down for a scheduled stop, I spotted a vending machine on the platform. On a whim, I grabbed my purse, jumped up and announced that I'd be right back.

"I'm just going to hop off and get a chocolate bar." I was gone before my mom even registered what I'd said.

In hindsight, I'm not sure why I thought this was a good idea, especially since as I stood in the bottleneck of people waiting to get off the train, a little voice in the back of my head was whispering, '*You probably won't have enough time now. You should probably just sit down.*' It was too late though; I was already mentally committed.

I jumped off the train and slid five euros into the vending machine. I was about to choose my chocolate bar when I heard the train doors close.

It couldn't be? Wasn't there a whistle? Where was the guy in the striped hat yelling "All Aboard?"

I quickly abandoned my five euros, ran back to the train and found that, sure enough, the doors were locked. I pressed the button outside the train. Nothing. Hopping up onto the step and banging on the glass, hoping to get someone's attention inside the train didn't help. A passenger on the other side of the glass put his hands up and shrugged his shoulders, indicating there was nothing he could do to help me.

All I could think about was that I'd left my mom and her sisters abandoned. I had the train tickets in my purse, along with the address of the villa. They knew it was somewhere in Tuscany, but I didn't even tell them the name of the town we were going to. All they knew was that they had to change trains in Bologna, but they didn't know where to go from there. No one had a phone that worked since they were overseas. My suitcase with all my belongings was inside the train. This could not be happening.

I had to think quickly. If this door didn't work, maybe another one would. I ran down to the next car and tried the same routine with no luck. As I stood on the step, with one arm holding the handrail and the other banging the window, the train started to move.

I was in shock.

What was I going to do? Without thinking my decision through (obviously), I decided the best option would be to hold on. I'd travelled through India; they did it all the time. How hard could it be, *right*?

The car I had attached myself to was near the end of the platform. As the train started picking up speed, I tightened my grasp and leaned in towards the train like a suction cup on a window. That's when I made eye contact with a man on the inside of the train that was waving his arms wildly in the air, motioning for me to get off the train, while doing hand gestures for 'Are you crazy?'

It wasn't until I was almost at the end of the very long platform that I realised how fast the train was now going, and that perhaps this was not a good idea. Before the platform disappeared I knew I had to jump, so I threw myself from the train onto the cement platform.

Since it was my first time jumping off a moving train, I didn't have a very good landing technique. I wish I could say I looked like Angelina Jolie in an action film, gracefully rolling from the train and landing without a scratch, but I definitely did not. If you've ever skipped rocks across water; that's what my body did across the cement.

The next thing I knew, two handsome Italian men picked me up off the ground, staring at me with eyes like saucers. They were saying a lot, and very quickly, again with hands flying in the air, but I understood none of it. From what I could make out, they wanted to bring me to the hospital, but all I could think of was that I need to get to Bologna as fast as possible. And also, that my favourite pants were completely shredded and the sunglasses that flew off my face were totalled.

Reluctantly, my newfound Italian friends put me in the only taxi that was willing to drive me to Bologna. I didn't know where I was, but from the expressions of every cab driver that denied them, I knew we weren't anywhere close to where I needed to be.

It wasn't until I was sitting alone in the back of the taxi that I came out of shock and assessed my damage, then, started sobbing hysterically. My pants were ripped open and my entire knee cap was an open wound, my opposite hip was gushing blood and I was pretty sure I might have broken my elbow. My immediate reaction was to call Kevin in Paris, not even registering the fact that I'd be delivering him this news while he was at work.

"You did WHAT?" he whisper-yelled into the phone.

Naively, I actually thought he might not have heard me the first time.

"I jumped off a train," I managed between sobs.

The conversation was a mix of emotions on his part. First there was panic, then worry, concern, relief, joy, followed by anger and finally frustration; your typical range of emotions for a weekday morning at ten a.m.

After I handed over a small mortgage payment to the taxi driver, I hobbled my way into the Bologna train station, literally looking like a train wreck, just in time to find my ladies on the platform, summoning the powers that be for a miracle. When they saw me limp over, their faces were all painted with, well actually, the same range of emotions as my earlier phone call.

Without having time to fully explain, they quickly tried to patch me up the best they could with what they had on hand: feminine hygiene products. Yes, indeed. I was gushing blood, and they were absorbent. Who was I to argue at this point? I got on the train covered in maxi pads and panty liners, happy to be alive.

My wonderful week in Tuscany consisted of lying on the couch, barely able to get clothes on over all the wounds, and unable to bend my knee and elbow. I walked around like the tin-man for the following month, housebound in Paris because I couldn't make it down the stairs at any of the Metro stations. It was all I could do to hobble back and forth to my *kiné* (physiotherapist) appointments every other day. Lesson learned: Do not jump from moving trains, no matter how bad you want a chocolate bar!

With my knee injury sealing my fate with the running group, I had to hang up my sneakers for a while. This left me with a big problem because I was living in a country that was renowned for their cuisine, wine, cheese, pastries, bread, the list goes on. Without running to balance my caloric intake versus exercise output, the scales were not evenly balanced, leaving my jeans a bit snug and creating the beginnings of a muffin top. How very unFrench of me!

At first I tried swimming because the French love their *natation*. Every doctor I saw and each *kiné* (physiotherapist) that worked on my knee, sent me directly to the pool. I needed to be doing low impact exercise that wasn't putting any stress on my knee joint, but I didn't really like swimming.

Correction. I didn't like swimming in a pool for exercise. Throw me on a beach in Bora Bora and I'll swim the day away in the ocean. But on an overcast, damp day in Paris, ask me to go to drag all my shower stuff to the public pool, don my swim cap and join the seniors for water aerobics. Well, that's just not quite as enticing.

I gave it a shot though because my calendar was wide open. I was soon a regular in the silver-haired group of ladies at the aquatics class two mornings a week. At ten thirty a.m. Tuesdays and Thursdays I'd be there, walking around the pool in circles, kicking my feet like part of the elderly school of fish. It wasn't my favourite activity, and I wasn't making any new friends besides the kinda slightly creepy lifeguard who was always overly eager to practise his English with me.

Abandoning the hope that swimming was going to diminish my muffin top, or more justly, croissant-top, I needed another option. I started going to different yoga classes around the city because at least I knew it was something I enjoyed. I was never completely dedicated to yoga, but I had gone to classes on and off for years. The problem was going to be getting through an entire yoga class in French.

After trying a few classes *en francais,* I was nearly ready to give up because the language barrier was doing the opposite of relaxing me. Then just in time, I found something promising online.

"Kev! All hope is not lost! I might not become morbidly obese after all," I shouted to him from the spare room. "And I might find people that speak English while I'm at it."

"What are you talking about?" He was trying to be patient with the fact that I'd just interrupted him watching the news for the fourth time in the last fifteen minutes to bring him 'news' of my own.

"I found a yoga studio in the Marais that has classes in English. It's not exactly in our neighbourhood, but it might be worth a shot?"

"You should check it out."

And with that, I grabbed my bag and scurried out the door to try and make it for the seven thirty class. Or should I say nineteen hours and thirty, because I was now trying to learn the twenty-four-hour clock, which was far too much like math for my liking.

"If I'm not back by ten p.m., come find me 'cause I'm lost," I shouted over my shoulder.

"You mean *vingt-deux heures*," I faintly heard him shout back the twenty-four hour clock as the door closed behind me, and I stepped into the elevator.

Namaste, Pass the Meat

The second I walked into this tiny yoga studio, I felt like I was home. I heard chatter coming from the changing area in French, and then, much to the delight of my ears, English.

It's not that I had a problem with people speaking French, I was living in France after all. But as an English speaker in a Francophone environment, I felt like an outsider so often. Even if I tried to follow a conversation, by the time I had worked out in my head what everyone was saying, then figured out the French words for what I wanted to contribute to the chat, the moment had long passed and I'd missed my opportunity, leaving me as the weird foreign mute, eavesdropping in on the conversation.

The worst was when everyone in a group of French speakers would laugh, and I was never sure if I should remain straight-faced, seeming miserable, or join in, falsely laughing, even though everyone knew I had no idea what I was laughing at. It was the height of social awkwardness.

That's why hearing English being spoken in the changing area of the yoga studio was like being wrapped in a warm hug. Knowing that I'd be able to speak to someone without struggling or sounding like I'd dropped out of school in the second grade made me instantly relax.

The owner of the studio and the teacher of our class that night came over to introduce herself. Add a bright ray of sunshine to the warm hug and you've got Michelle: a New Yorker transplanted in Paris, spreading the yoga love, one class at a time.

By the end of the class I knew I'd be back, whether the studio was in our neighbourhood or not; I finally had found somewhere I fit in. I grabbed a pamphlet on the way out at the end of class, slipped it into my bag and headed towards the Metro, yoga mat tucked under my arm, where if I were really French, I'd have my baguette.

I didn't know it then, but soon I'd be able to do that route without even thinking of where I was going. I'd even come to know exactly which end of each Metro platform to stand on to shave off a few seconds off my line changes.

The Metro wasn't that busy at that time in the evening, so I scored two empty seats: one for me and one for my yoga mat and bag. I got comfortable and dug into my bag looking for the paper I took on the way out, wanting to know more about the studio I was at. On the back side, a piece of paper attached with a staple spoke to me.

Yoga Teacher Training
6 months
2500 euros

Sirens went off in my mind and imaginary red lights started flashing. This was it! This is what I needed to do with myself in Paris.

I was already a teacher, so why not become a yoga teacher.

Small problem being: I had no income to pay for this course.

"I need two thousand five hundred euros," came spilling out of my mouth as soon as I opened our apartment door. This was quickly followed by me biting my bottom lip because as soon as it escaped my mouth, I didn't like the way it sounded. I didn't mean to be so blunt, but I was just too excited to contain myself.

I was met with a confused look.

"Hi, love, how was yoga and why do you need two thousand five hundred euros?" In spite of living in Paris, we were fairly new to the country and still converted to Canadian dollars in our minds, especially for a big-ticket item like that. Kevin was good at math and it didn't take him long to realise this was a lot of money, especially since we had recently become a single-income family.

We talked about it and agreed that if this is what I really wanted to do, we'd find a way to make it work.

The course started in January and would last until June. It would have me practising yoga a couple times throughout the week, and studying theory all weekend. It was a huge time commitment, but Kevin's job had him working on a second master's degree, at a prestigious, *'Grande Ecole'* in Paris so he would also be busy studying on the weekends. This just might work.

The girls in the yoga teacher training were fabulous. A mix of anglophones and francophones, but the theory was taught in English. We were all so different, but somehow we fit together perfectly. And best of all, I loved being back in part of a sisterhood. My heart was quickly full.

If someone passed me on the street, I likely wouldn't strike them as a yogini. I'm fit, but not thin and willowy, like the picture I have in my mind of women who teach yoga. I'm not the best in the class, I can't do a headstand, and I am most definitely not a vegetarian. In fact, I didn't even know that being vegetarian was part of practising yoga until I learned it the hard, embarrassing way.

The training hadn't started yet, but I had become a regular at the studio. One night after class, we all decided to go out for dinner at a cute place around the corner. We settled in, tucked our mats in the corner and started to scan the menus. After being at French class earlier that day, talking about food, then burning energy at a yoga class, I was starving.

I didn't pay attention to what everyone else was ordering because I was in my own world, zoned in on the menu. Without Kevin across the table, I was left to painfully translate each word on the menu in my head, trying to figure out what I was going to have.

"Tartare de boeuf s'il vous plait," I told the waiter in my best French.

When I first arrived in Paris the thought of eating raw ground beef with some spices and a raw egg mixed in was enough to make me gag. But Kevin ordered it regularly, and after watching him eat it a few times, he finally persuaded me to give it a taste. It had slowly grown on me, each time tasting a bit more, until he finally said I'd have to start ordering my own. Maybe I was slowly integrating into my surroundings after all.

Think again.

When the food arrived I glanced around the table, desperately hoping I wouldn't have food envy. First a quiche. No worries there. Then came the *Courgette Lasagne.* If I was going to have the calories that come with lasagna, I'd prefer the real thing, not zucchini noodles. *Salade Chèvre Chaud* was placed across from me. As much as I loved warm goat cheese salad, I was way too hungry for that. More quiche and another salad left the kitchen and landed on our table. There was no food envy so far, but I was starting to notice a pattern.

There was nothing on the table that was once a living thing. I wanted to curl up in a ball and roll myself out of the restaurant when it hit me. They're yoginis. Of course! They are all vegetarians. I was mortified.

And about two seconds after I realised there was a food trend I was not a part of, my pile of raw beef was placed on the table in front of me. Could there possibly be a worse thing than steak tartare to order at a table full of non-meat eaters? A chicken sandwich would have been tolerable. Even a steak would have even been okay. But instead arrived a small mountain of uncooked beef topped with a runny, raw egg, and it sat in the middle of a table full of people whose stomachs were probably turning at the sight of it. It was a horrible moment to be me.

How was I going to handle this *faux pas*? I could play dumb, call the waiter back and tell him he must have misunderstood my French, insisting I said, '*Quiche*' not '*Tartare de Boeuf*'. That would be a stretch. I could ignore that there was a very awkward situation on our hands and just quietly eat my dinner. Or maybe my best option was to just bolt out the door of the *petite* brasserie and never show my face at that yoga studio again. I was way too hungry for the last option.

I decided my only choice was to be myself, and at least they all spoke English, so I could do that a lot easier.

"Shit. You guys are all vegetarians, aren't you?" I scrunched up my face and pulled my best apologetic smile.

Breaking awkward moments with humour was my *forté*, and I managed to get a few laughs by pointing out the grave contrast in our orders. My new friends assured me it was okay that I ate meat and I wasn't kicked out of the 'club'.

In hindsight I think it was better that way. It was early on in our friendship and had I realised it ahead of time, had I found out another way, I may have felt the pressure and pulled the 'of course I'm a vegetarian too' card, like a teenager wanting to fit in with the cool kids at a high school dance.

The girls still liked me, even though I clearly didn't follow a yoga diet. And for that, I loved them. I officially had some friends!

Vin Chaud

It was Christmas time in Paris and I had turned into a hopeless romantic.

The streets were lined with decorations and festive lights shone bright from the lamp posts each night. I had discovered my love of *vin chaud*, and it had become somewhat of a tradition for Kevin and I to roam the streets on the weekends and end our evenings sipping on my new favourite drink, hot wine. I was aware that the Brits drank it, referring to it as 'mulled wine' but I couldn't figure out how this had not caught on in Canada. The country has the market cornered on cold weather, next to Russia of course, but at least the Russians had vodka to keep them warm. *Vin chaud* could have completely changed my view on outdoor activities in the Canadian winter.

Since I wasn't working and mainly spent my time going between French class and the yoga studio, I passed a lot of time walking through Paris, checking out every hidden corner between the two places. The month of December brought a jackpot of oddities in the city my way.

Early in the month I ran into the paparazzi for the first time in my life.

I was hunting down a recommended jeweller to get my wedding ring resized. I came out of the jewellery shop and was sweating after glancing down at the bill for the size adjustment. This swanky neighbourhood was way outside my price range and that was confirmed again two seconds later when I found out Katy Perry was shopping next door. I didn't actually know what was going on, nor had I ever seen the paparazzi in action before. But when I left the jewellers and was battered by a flutter of camera flashes that obviously weren't for me, I simply walked up to one of the camera men, without realising I was blocking his shot, and asked what was going on.

"Katie Perry," he motioned into the store, "she is doing zee shopping."

"Well, I guess she's gotta buy Christmas presents too!" was the only response I could think of, and I merrily went on my way. But not before catching a glance of her through the glass front of the store. As I walked away, I pulled out my phone to google who Katy Perry actually was since I've never been one for following celebrities.

In mid-December I surprised Kevin with a piece of cake from the world's longest *buche de Noel*.

"The *world's* longest? Is it possible that you might be exaggerating?" he questioned as I passed him a slice after dinner.

"Nope. I'm not. They had a display set up at La Défense, with tables pushed together that winded back and forth like a snake to display the Christmas log. When it was finally all set out, there was a representative from *The Guinness Book of World Records* to measure the cake and then there was a big celebration. I showed up just as they were finishing and handing out pieces to go."

"Nice timing," he retorted.

Paris was chalked full of surprises. There were Santa runs and Christmas parades where thousands of people would dress up in red Santa suits and take to the streets, some armed with music and others with wine. If you didn't know about the event you'd be going about your merry way and suddenly be crossed with an army of St Nicholases flooding the streets. I wasn't one of the people surprised by this though because I was a participant.

I was asked to go by a girl who also takes French classes in the building I do, and since Kevin wasn't going to be home until later that evening and I had nothing else planned, I said yes. We went to the grocery store, and found some cheap felt Santa outfits that were being sold for ten euros. Once we were suited up, we joined the other masses of Santas that were spreading Christmas cheer while dancing through the streets. People randomly joined along with nearly full orchestras playing Christmas music and one Santa who actually brought a twelve-pack of wine glasses and was passing them out to people around him, filling them up as he went along. Now there's a great way to make new friends. We popped into the Monoprix as we passed by, grabbed a bottle of red and ran back out to our place in the parade of Santas.

What amazed me most about the ability to drink in public in Paris was that it never seemed to be abused. People always had wine in parks, and now we were parading through the streets with actual *glass* wine glasses, yet, no one took it as an opportunity to get drunk. Binge drinking was not part of the culture. Chalk it up to being uncivilised, and thus, unFrench, I suppose.

With all the fun that came with Christmas in Paris, there was nothing I loved more than the Christmas markets.

The *Marché de Noel* had me once again shaking my head in disbelief that this was not a 'thing' at home. The two big Christmas markets that we would tend to go to were on the Champs-Élysées, and at La Défense, which is the business district of Paris. These had enough space to have giant markets, but there were other smaller markets set up throughout the city too.

As we walked up, hand in hand, through the *Marché de Noel* I was gushing. "Isn't it so romantic, Kev?"

"I suppose it is." He laughed at me, not being much of a romantic himself.

I took in my surroundings like a child at the circus for the first time. There were little cabins set up, one beside the other, each housing different items to either eat, drink, or buy as Christmas presents. Gift choices were an array of hats and mitts, handmade soaps, scented oils, Paris souvenirs, wooden toys for kids, and Christmas decorations.

"Now that's romantic!" Kevin joked as he motioned towards the cabin selling sexy Santa-inspired lingerie. I nudged him in the ribs, and we kept walking.

"Let's go find a *vin chaud*." I was ready to warm up. Even though it wasn't anywhere near the December temperatures I was used to, I never spent this much time walking around outside at this time of year back home.

It didn't take long to find a stall selling wine since from six cabins down, we could hear a man in a deep voice repeatedly yelling out, "*Chaud, chaud, le vin chaud!*" He might as well have been calling my name. I was his target audience and was now making a bee-line right towards him.

"It reminds me of a carnival the way he's shouting out," I told Kevin. "But instead of 'Get your popcorn!' he's yelling, 'Get your wine!' What could be better? I love this place!"

"*Deux vins chaud, s'il vous plait, Monsieur!*" I requested with more pep than any French person ever would.

He handed us our glasses, and I let out a quiet purr when the warm wine hit my cold lips.

"Have I mentioned I love this place?" I smiled.

"The place or the wine?" he asked, smirking.

"Both."

We continued to peruse the market and decided we'd have dinner there. We had so many choices and so much to learn since a lot of the food was new to us.

Snacks at the market were plentiful: from savoury items like cheese, cured meat, roasted chestnuts, and pretzels, to sweets like crepes, *beignets*(doughnuts), *gaufres*(waffles), nougat, canelé, macarons, hand-made chocolates and churros.

For dinner there were some tables set up where you could sit while you feasted. We first spotted sausages and sauerkraut that was being cooked on frying pans that were bigger than my outstretched arms. "That's a perfect portion size for you," I joked.

We carried on past stands with roasted pork, pulled pork, chicken drumsticks, and duck.

"Whatever that is, I want it!" I dragged Kevin by the hand towards the giant wheel of cheese I saw oozing onto bread.

"*C'est Raclette*," the woman answered the question she could tell I was about to ask.

The large wheel of cheese was propped up under a broiler. The exposed side of the cheese round was melting into a wonderful, gooey cheese heaven, that was then scraped off onto a baguette. I needed to look no further.

Kevin wasn't feeling very gastronomically adventurous and ordered a cheese sausage on a bun. But he also couldn't resist sharing a *tartiflette* with me. We were served a small container of sliced potatoes, baked with cream, chunks of bacon, and cheese. Totally full, we washed it all down with one more *vin chaud* and started walking back to our apartment as we finished our wine.

"This country is going to make me fat," I announced as I flopped myself onto our bed later that night.

Kevin turned the handles on the windows and pulled them into the house. It was still strange for me that there were no screens. He stuck his body through the window outside and reached around, unlatching the shutters. Before he pulled the shutters in and locked them, he breathed in the crisp winter air and then out of nowhere shouted out for all of Paris to hear, "*Chaud, chaud, le vin chaud!*" in the exact same booming voice as the Frenchman at the *Marché de Noel*.

He caught me so off guard that I burst out laughing, barely able to contain myself. Maybe it was that last glass of *vin chaud* that made me think it was so funny. But had I known that he would then think it was funny to start regularly yelling that out into the streets of Paris when he closed the shutters at night, I may have tried to curb my laughter.

Baguette in the Oven

It was only two weeks into my six-month yoga training, and I had to have a sit down with my teacher, Michelle, and ask her if I needed to quit.

"I'm pregnant," I told her before the other girls arrived.

Her face lit up the room. "Lisa, that's fantastic!"

Kevin and I always knew that we wanted kids, but we hadn't ever discussed when it would actually happen until we arrived in Paris. Since I was thirty, and no longer working, it felt like the right time to make it happen.

"So, I can stay?" I asked unsure what the policy was on pregnancy and teacher training. I hadn't been pregnant before, but I knew I had no intentions of doing any handstands with a baby in my belly. I was far too uncoordinated for that.

"Of course you can stay! You've got life growing inside of you. What a beautiful miracle," she said as she wrapped me up in a giant hug.

It was still early days, so after confirming with Michelle that I could stay in the training, I let her know that I would keep my pregnancy quiet for the standard first couple of months. But this baby wanted to be seen and was quickly popping.

Being pregnant in Paris was amazing! Not only was I always offered a seat on the Metro, and I never had to wait in line anywhere (including the grocery store), but the best, and most obvious part was that I was surrounded by heavenly *boulangeries, patisseries,* and *chocolatiers.* My baby was living a foodie's dream via my umbilical cord!

As the days rolled on, there was no more hiding my growing belly under the tight lycra of my yoga clothes. Not to mention I was sure that my new friends in the course must have been noticing that I was modifying all the poses and twists that weren't prenatal friendly. Yet, when I announced my upcoming bundle of joy, the news seemed to come as a shock to them, and they were genuinely excited for me and the journey we'd be taking together.

It was so nice to have people to share my news with. I may not have had my family or my old friends nearby to rub my belly, but week after week, my yoga girls watched me grow, rubbed my belly and cared for my baby and I with all of the love and light they had, which was a lot. I was grateful to have them. These women had become my new friends in Paris and they were quickly becoming my family in this foreign land where family was one thing I was seriously lacking.

I suppose that's what happens when you spend countless hours with people whose company you mutually enjoy. We practised yoga together, ate together and spent time together after class. My new yoga friends took care of me as my family would have if they had been around. Every Sunday between morning theory class and afternoon practical, we would lay out a giant spread of Parisian-style picnic in the middle of the yoga studio, or if the weather permitted, in nearby parks.

During our weekly picnics they would go out of their way to track down pasteurised cheese (no easy task in France) and make sure our lunches were always pregnancy friendly. Opening the flap of their picnic baskets revealed new treasures that my North American taste buds came to love. From savoury tarts, to delicious salads, it seemed like these women could take the simplest ingredients and bring them to life with their inherited French touch. Their carefully crafted meals and offering of pasteurised cheeses were most definitely received as a token of their affection.

Part of our training had us spending the weekend at a yoga retreat centre in the middle of France. Embracing my inner hippy, I was ready to take everything I knew about ashrams, which was solely what Julia Roberts depicted in *Eat, Pray, Love,* and come back to Paris refreshed, rejuvenated and glowing.

The first night we were there, the sound of an alarm going off jerked me out of a deep sleep.

My eyes squinted around the room to try and place where I was and what the horrific sound was piercing my ears. It didn't take long before I clued in that I was at the ashram and the high-pitched noise pollution was an alarm clock, something I hadn't used in many months. My hand feverishly searched the clock in search of the off switch.

Five thirty was the time staring back at me. *Holy crap that is early!* I was probably more familiar with using that hour as a bedtime, not a wake up time! I scraped my body out of bed and my bare feet padded down the hall, eyes still half-closed, as I made my way to the bathroom. Suddenly the nine o'clock start of my old running group didn't seem so bad.

The bathroom was dark at five thirty in the morning and I wasn't ready to turn on the light. I was about to sit down on the toilet in the dimly lit room, when I glanced down and was stopped in my tracks by the bloated state of my stomach. *What on earth did I eat?* I was completely swollen! And then, two or three very long seconds later, I remembered I was pregnant. I still wasn't used to my changing body and being out of my element at a ridiculously early hour (or late, depending how you look at it) completely caught me off guard.

Even though we woke up before the sun each day, the weekend was relaxing. We practiced yoga, studied for our exams, and shared meals together (all vegetarian, of course). I may have lost a few hours of early morning sleep, but I would soon come to know those wee hours of the morning all too well.

I felt great throughout my pregnancy. This probably had a lot to do with the amount of yoga I did and the fact that I walked everywhere I went. It also helped that French men have no qualms about hitting on pregnant women. I learned that even with my wedding ring shining brightly on my ring finger and belly protruding through my shirt, French men would still be stereotypical French men. You've gotta love them for it. And I'm not really complaining because it was great for my self-esteem.

"As if you can turn heads while you're six months pregnant," my friend Carol said to me as we were walking by a terrace full of lunch-time diners down the street from her apartment in Neuilly.

"Are you insane? Men don't check out pregnant chicks. That's just wrong." I snarled at her in fake disgust. "We're basically invisible. There's nothing sexy about this." I motioned to my body.

"Well, I just saw it happen when you walked by that table full of guys." She motioned with her head to the table we just passed.

I took a quick look over my shoulder in the direction she was nodding and sure enough, there was a table of men on their standard two and a half-hour lunch break, giving me the eyes, and actually smiled at me proudly when I busted them.

"Told you!" Carol beamed.

"That's crazy! Must be my new boobs this pregnancy has given me," I joked, since she had just come with me a few days earlier to buy bigger bras.

I wish I could tell you that it only happened that once. But I remember several different instances while being pregnant in Paris where I had overly interested men in my presence. It was a bit disturbing, but to be honest, even pregnant women appreciate having that, *'still got it'* feeling. So I chalked it up as a compliment, because I wasn't getting very many on my ability to speak French gracefully.

All the modifications that I had to learn in yoga because I was pregnant made me the perfect person to substitute teach for prenatal classes at the yoga studio. At this point I had all my hours, I just needed to write my exam, so I felt confident enough to step up when they needed me to take over a class.

I was at home trying to memorise the Sanskrit terms I needed for my final exam (because learning French isn't hard enough, I might as well throw some Sanskrit in there too) when my phone rang. One of the girls at the studio needed me to go teach prenatal that night. I was free, as usual, and I told her it was no problem.

I arrived early, and got ready for the fellow future *Mamans* to arrive.

As the ladies started arriving, they were genuinely pleased to see that I too had a belly of my own. I was greeted with, *"Bonjour"* several times, but that wasn't alarming because we were in Paris after all. What did set off the alarm bells was when one of the girls turned to me and said, *"Cette classe est en francais, oui?"*

What? Let me think about that. Would I be teaching the class in French? NO!!

"Pardon?" I asked her to repeat herself in order to buy myself some time to compose a response while I completely panicked inside.

"Normalement cette classe est en français." She repeated that the class was normally in French.

You'd think that the fact that I was expected to teach an entire class, for ninety minutes in French might have been mentioned by the teacher I was replacing. All my zen went out the window at that moment and I instantly broke into a cold sweat. How was I going to get out of this one?

"Bien sur." I told her that *of course* the class would be taught in French because that seemed like the proper response even though I had no ability to conduct a class in the language of her preference.

I was sweating heavily before I even hit the yoga mat, and my only saving grace was imagining Kevin's face when I went home and told him about the situation I was in with these Parisienne women. He would be speechless.

Luckily the ladies were kind, as yoginis tend to be, and it didn't take them long to see just how badly I was struggling with anatomy in French. My time living in Paris meant that I could now order the hell out of a glass of red wine *en francais*, but trying to tell someone to engage their pelvic floor was a very different story. We got through the very humbling experience with a combination of Franglish and charades, my personal specialty. I'd like to think it wasn't as bad as I remember, but it probably was.

The Move

It was late spring in Paris; birds were chirping, tulips were in full bloom and the tourists were arriving *en masse*.

Everyone knows Parisians have a bad reputation about being rude to tourists. Personally, I don't think they deserve it, but maybe living in the city turned me into a bit of a Parisian snob myself. When spring came around, tourists seemed to be everywhere I went and I could understand why the locals were annoyed; all these extra people messed with my daily routine.

It was Saturday morning and I was on my way to the yoga studio. This Saturday was particularly important because we had our anatomy exam, and my friend Sharon was doing her final exam. She'd be teaching a class while being graded, and I didn't want to be rude and stroll in late.

When I left the house I wasn't worried about how much time I had because I had my commute for getting to the studio down to a science. Unless there was transportation strike, (which was fairly common in France) I would be right on time and could get a few extra minutes of studying in on the way there. Yoga mat in hand, I headed to the Metro.

When I got underground I couldn't even recognise my own neighbourhood. There were people everywhere. I could barely get myself squeezed into one of the cars when the Metro pulled up. All of a sudden I was surrounded by English speakers, loud English speakers. With giant backpacks, banging into me from every which way.

There's a precision and flow to public transit in Paris, just as there is to any other routine that you do daily. The unwritten rules to this daily ritual are: doors open, those waiting to get on stand to the sides, allowing those on the train to exit, the new passengers file in, filling the seats, then standing room, leaving the area by the door for the last-minute dare devils that try to sneak in as the door is about to close. It runs like a well-oiled machine, until the tourists arrive.

Of course Paris has tourists all year long, but it seems like the influx in late spring is so great that they almost take over. People try to get on the Metro while the passengers haven't even gotten off yet, causing a traffic jam. They stand right in front of the door, not leaving room for others to get on, or they exit and stand on the platform right in front of the door, deciding which way to go. I understand that people might be nervous about riding public transportation in a foreign country, and they want to take a little extra time to make sure they're in the right spot. They have every right to do that, but when a regular passenger is trying to get to work, or say for example, an anatomy exam, a group of people standing in front of the door double-checking their location, making it impossible to get in, resulting in having to wait for the next train, it's a little frustrating for a pregnant lady running late. Just saying, I get where the Parisians are coming from on the tourist front.

When I finally got myself squeezed in, there were so many people that I could barely move. The loud-talking English speakers were not giving me the warm-fuzzies that I usually get when I overhear people speaking my mother-tongue. Normally, my ears could pick up an English speaker from two aisles over in the grocery store and it always put a little smile on my face, making me feel like I wasn't alone. But these particular people were of the loud, over excited variety, and I was planning on using the ride to study for my anatomy exam. After several attempts of looking down at my paper, but being bumped around by tourists not wanting to hold the hand rails, I finally gave up my attempt with a loud sigh. I really was becoming French.

It wasn't the tourists' fault. They were excited, as they should be. It was Paris! But when a normal walk through Chatelet Station is taken over by hordes of loud college kids on their Euro-backpacking tour, those of us trying to carry on with our everyday programming tend to get slightly irritated. I felt this way and I was fairly new to Paris; I can't imagine how the veterans felt. It explains why the month of August is almost barren of actual Parisians. They all flee for their one-month vacation, leaving the tourists to have their way with the city in their absence.

After navigating through the tourist mob, I managed to make it to Sharon's class just in time. Although my glowing, pregnant-lady aura was left behind on the Metro.

Nearing the end of my pregnancy, I could seriously notice the difference in my body. Not only the blooming belly under my imported Lululemon activewear, but all the yoga had transformed the rest of my body as well. I felt like I was stronger at seven months pregnant than I was the day I signed up for the course.

I was feeling really calm about the whole pregnancy experience. My yoga classes also consisted of *pranayama,* which are breathing techniques and meditation sessions, which were both new for someone like myself, whose prior yoga experience mainly consisted of classes taken at the gym; no meditating involved aside from the concentration it took to block out the sound of the pulsing base coming from the techno music blasting in the main area of the building.

So I had transferred over to the 'other side'. I was a yogini now, walking through the streets of Paris, baguette under one arm and yoga mat under the other. There was an aura glowing around me, not only because of the pregnancy, but because I had become so 'zen' about my new yoga-filled lifestyle that I felt like I could breathe my way through any problem life threw my way.

Just as I sent that thought out to the universe, I swear I heard a little bit of laughter off in the distance.

I walked in the door after yoga that night and Kevin asked what I thought about moving.

"What do you mean?" I questioned back, rubbing my enormous belly. Surely he couldn't have meant any time soon, I was in my third trimester.

"Soon," he said, almost reading my mind. "It would have to be soon, so we can settle in before the baby comes."

"BEFORE?" The words escaped my mouth louder than I meant for them to. "How can we possibly move *before* the baby comes?"

He paused for a moment, and I wasn't sure if he was gathering his thoughts, or convincing himself that this could work. "We've talked about living in the south of France. Life would be quieter, we'd have a house, a car and a yard. It would be more like the kind of life we're used to." He raised his eyebrows and looked to me for confirmation of his sentiment.

I nodded and he continued. "Well, I was in a meeting today and they proposed we go. It would probably be for three or four years, and we'd have to leave right away because of the baby."

"There'd be movers to take care of all the packing, so there wouldn't really be any stress," he added, again knowing I was trying to work out the logistics in my mind.

Moving to a place I'd never even visited, in a country that was still fairly foreign to me, that late in a pregnancy seemed a bit crazy. Would I be able to breathe my way through *that*?

I agreed with the principle that our lifestyle would be more like the one we knew back home, so we accepted the offer. I tried to use my newfound yogi attitude to remain 'chill' about the whole thing. But France is known for its mountains of paper work, and moving to the most southern point of the country left a paper trail that nightmares were made of. There were packers and moving trucks on the Paris side of things. I got through that okay. But now we actually had to *get* to the south of France!

"I'm nearly eight months pregnant, can I even fly?" I questioned Kevin over dinner one night.

"We'll just put you in one of my hockey jerseys and hope they'll let you on the plane." Typical Canadian-guy thing to say. "It's a short flight, only an hour away. You'll be okay," he offered as a consolation when he noticed I wasn't loving his first response.

The following weekend, after a long day on the yoga mat I met up with Kevin for a date, just as we always did after my Saturday class. As usual, I had the appetite of a pregnant lady who had just spent eight hours in a yoga studio. Even if a lot of that time was studying a textbook, and not actually practising yoga, I didn't have easy access to a fridge, or a snack cupboard.

"J'ai faim!" I announced my hunger in French to get a smile out of Kevin as I saw him waiting for me outside the Metro.

"I figured you might be." He returned the smile, grabbing my hand and throwing my bag full of books over his shoulder.

That night at dinner we discussed our impending move. We now knew for certain that we'd soon be saying goodbye to the city of lights. Kevin accepted the offer with work, and we were mentally preparing for a move to the south of France that upcoming summer.

We had mixed feelings as we'd now really fallen in love with Paris and all its little quirks. As much as we'd miss the romance of it all, there was also something quite appealing about the idea of having our baby in small-town southern France and the slower pace of life that came with it. I was looking forward to getting back some of the conveniences we didn't have in Paris, like having a house and a car. No more carrying my groceries home. And of course I couldn't wait for the food. The food is amazing all over France but everyone who heard we were moving south, immediately said, *"Vous allez bien manger,"* assuring us we'd be eating well there. It was the home of foie gras, Béarnaise sauce, cured meats, stinky cheese, and duck everything.

The moment we told our family and friends we'd be leaving Paris, flights instantly began getting booked. Everyone wanted to get a visit in before we checked out. We saw parents, cousins, friends, old high school acquaintances, and ex-girlfriends of old high school acquaintances, all in a very short time frame.

Not working during the day meant that I was a tour guide for many guests passing through. I loved walking around Paris, so I didn't mind, and even though I was pregnant I can proudly say that I climbed the stairs of the Eiffel Tower more times than I can remember.

My favourite place to bring our visitors was for a stroll down rue Cler. It's right around the corner from the Eiffel Tower and it's full of cute little shops selling cheese and meat, wine, fruit and there's places to stop for a bite to eat. The restaurants weren't fancy, but there was one particular place where I loved going for a lunchtime pizza. It was when my father-in-law visited that I realised I had become a regular, and I wondered what the restaurant staff thought of me.

My mom had just been in Paris with her sisters earlier in the year and Kevin's mom was still working, so she couldn't make the visit. This left my dad on a solo visit, followed a few hours later by Kevin's dad. They literally passed at the airport, leaving just enough time for me to wash the sheets on the pull-out couch.

It was great to be able to show our dads around Paris, but as I bit into my piping hot pizza on rue Cler, I caught a look in our waiter's eye. He recognised me, which wasn't surprising. I was heavily pregnant, an obvious foreigner, with terrible French, but not a tourist because I was in there too often. But the look that flashed across this face was more than just recognising me as a regular.

"Oh man, Kev, it was so embarrassing! He totally thought I was *with* your dad!"

"You don't know that for sure." He couldn't hide his amused smirk.

"I *totally* know that for sure because I saw his face! He thought your dad and I were an item, and I could tell he remembered me from earlier in the week being there with my dad. He thinks I'm into old guys."

My volume was rising as I recounted the story. "And not just one old guy, but several. He probably thinks I was cheating on my dad with your dad and wondering which one is the father of my baby. It's too much to think about!" I shouted, flopping back onto the bed and covering my face with a pillow.

"Don't worry," Kevin halfheartedly tried to console me, "my dad was the last old guy you'll have to date for a while."

The Last Supper

"Is *vingt et un heure* okay for dinner tonight?" Kevin asked, tongue firmly pressed in cheek to stifle his smirk, knowing I hated the twenty-four-hour clock.

He knew how to press my buttons. If it wasn't bad enough that he was speaking to me in twenty-four-hour clock; he was speaking to me in the French twenty-four hour clock. That was a lot of code for me to crack before I could answer his question.

"Ya, eight is fine." I finally got around to answering once I did the translation and math in my head.

"I can't believe you still need to count the hours on your fingers," he playfully shook his head in my direction.

It was true. I still had to use my fingers to figure out anything after noon.

One finger = 1:00 = 13hr

Two fingers = 2:00 = 14hr

Three fingers = 3:00 = 15hr

It was fairly elementary, but it was the only way I could wrap my mind around it. French was hard enough, but throwing math in there was just plain mean of this country I was living in. I'll never forget the first time I woke up from a deep sleep and glanced at the clock to see it read 00:10.

What the hell time is that? I was in a sleepy fog and it took far too long to figure out if it was the middle of the night or if I'd just fallen asleep for a pregnancy nap.

As the clock crept up on twenty-one hours I started grilling Kevin about dinner.

"Come on, just tell me where we're going," I whined, hoping to crack him, but not succeeding.

"Nope. You'll find out when we get there. That's why it's called a surprise."

Most of our things were packed up and ready for the movers so this would be one of our last nights out for a romantic dinner in Paris. We made our way outside where we walked the cobblestone, hand in hand, enjoying the perfectly comfortable silence, both taking in our adoptive city in all her glory. We knew we were thinking the same thing.

"I'm going to miss this," Kevin said to me, breaking the silence.

"Me too," I admitted. "I bet you'd never thought you'd hear me say that," I said with a little laugh.

The truth was, I really *would* miss Paris. Although I tried my best to jump right into life in Paris when we arrived, I couldn't help but spend part of that time mourning my old life instead of appreciating what I had right in front of me. Paris! Just when I was feeling settled, we were about to start over. I made a mental note to live in the moment and I planned to enjoy every last one I had in the city.

"This is the place," Kevin announced as our stroll came to a stop in front of a restaurant with a sign reading *'Dans La Noir'*.

"In the Black," I unnecessarily translated the sign for my francophone husband.

He brought me into a restaurant where the concept was eating in the dark. My first thoughts were that the food must have been really bad if they didn't want anyone to see it. But Kevin assured me that it was the contrary. They felt that their food would be even more enhanced if you used only your sense of smell and taste. Apparently he'd heard good things about it so we gave it a shot.

"Tell them I'm pregnant," I nudged him. "I don't want to eat anything weird."

"I think they can tell you're pregnant, Lis."

Fair enough. There was no hiding my protruding belly at this point. According to the weekly emails I was receiving, the baby was the size of an eggplant but I'd guess more like a large watermelon by the looks of me. I wasn't sure how French women, usually petite to start with, managed to stay tiny during pregnancy. Every pregnant French woman I saw stayed her same size, but with a neatly placed volleyball under her shirt. I was starting to look pregnant everywhere; my cheeks were becoming pregnant, my upper arms, and definitely my thighs. Under my shirt there wasn't a volleyball, or even a basketball. I most definitely was hiding something more along the lines of a beachball, and I had a couple of months to go.

After the waitress confirmed that indeed I was pregnant, she asked if there was anything I couldn't eat, and I gave her the standard pregnancy list, then we were all set to go.

I wasn't sure how eating in the dark would actually work. Were we going to wear blindfolds? Or was it just going to be really dim lighting?

We were brought to a section in the main entrance where we were given a locker to put our belongings. This was just before the days where it became mandatory to take a picture of your food before you ate it, so not having a camera or phone at the table didn't faze us.

From there, we were led from the front room into complete and utter darkness. It was impossible to see anything at all. Whether my eyes were open or closed made no difference. Had I known I'd be spending the night in the pinch-black, I would have stayed in my joggers and lost the heels. It would have been a lot more comfortable than the fitted maternity dress I had wiggled my way into.

I was holding onto the shoulder of the hostess who was guiding us to our table, and Kevin was holding my hand, following close behind me. When the little train we created came to a stop, we were carefully led to our seats at a table that could have either been fit for a queen, or resembled a low-budget burger joint. I had no idea because I couldn't see a thing. The bill we received at the end of the night, however, confirmed that it was not a burger joint.

We weren't alone at our table in the dark. It was group seating, which I assume was to make navigating the restaurant in the dark easier for everyone. The shared tables didn't faze us much because in Parisian restaurants the tables were so close together you were practically sitting with other people anyway.

"*Bonsoir,*" I was greeted by the man sitting beside me.

Great. This guy was going to want to make polite small talk in French all night and I wouldn't even be able to do my standard smile-and-nod move because he wouldn't be able to see me.

"*Bonsoir, monsieur,*" I replied with a polite smile that he couldn't see. I wanted to make a joke about how he really drew the short straw being seated beside me because I wouldn't be much of a conversationalist, but I couldn't find the words under the pressure, so I just stayed quiet and let him assume I was either shy or unsociable instead of just a foreigner with a limited vocabulary.

As our food came I was unsure. Kevin loved it because it was different, but I was a tougher sell. Tastes and textures can be a strange and touchy thing for pregnant women. Being presented with a plate of food that you couldn't see and instead you have to try and guess what you're eating wasn't my favourite thing. Except for dessert, of course. I had no issues firing that down the hatch without hesitation.

I liked the idea of the restaurant. It was definitely an 'experience' and the fact that they employed visually impaired service staff was bonus points in their direction. But the whole eating-in-the-dark business would be something I'd take a pass on next time. Or at least until I was able to swallow mystery seafood without setting off my gag reflex.

Walking back home, we did our standard loop by the Eiffel Tower because too soon that would no longer be an option.

"Should we hang around a bit until it starts to twinkle?" Kevin looked my way, already knowing my answer.

And we waited until the top of the hour when we soaked up our last visit to the *Tour Eiffel* as local residents.

Chez Webb

Once we'd made the leap to move to France, and accepted all that went with that, moving from Paris to the south of France was easier than a trip to the dentist. The adjustment period of living in the country had passed, and although the language barrier didn't seem to be going anywhere quickly, I was already used to dealing with it. All the big life changes were already done the year before, so this move felt like a breeze.

We relocated to Pau, in the Bearn province of France, nestled at the foot of the Pyrenees Mountains. The city was home to about eighty thousand people and acted as the main hub in the area. Many small villages very closely surrounded Pau, running into each other to make up the region. We were about an hour's drive to the Atlantic coast, and twenty minutes further would have us in Spain. In the other direction we were almost stumbling distance to Bordeaux. But this was all hearsay while we were in Paris because I'd never actually been there until I landed there with my giant belly, ready to call this place I'd never seen, home.

I was just at the beginning of my eighth month of pregnancy, but since it wasn't an international flight, the airline barely seemed to notice I was pregnant, even though my stomach was the size of a full blown beach ball. I lost count of the number of times French people had asked if I was having twins. *Jumeaux* was the French word for twins, and although I wasn't having them, the size of my belly made the word a regular part of my vocabulary.

Moving to a new city without visiting it first was actually sitting quite fine with me. If I could move myself across the ocean and commit to living in an apartment I'd never seen before, I could easily move a few hours away. My main concern was finding a home quickly because as much as I love the story of Christmas, I didn't want my baby to be born in a barn. I was eight months pregnant, and I wanted a home. Immediately.

The real estate agent who brought us to visit the houses caught a glimpse of me as I exited the car; his eyes nearly bulged out of his head.

"I see you're going to need a home soon!" he emphasised *soon* as his eyes veered toward my midsection. I smile politely, and wish my French was polished enough for a witty remark like I would have thought of in English.

In Paris I had some awkward moments because of my lack of French, but generally speaking, the city is so used to having tourists that a person can get by without speaking a ton of French. More times than I'd like to admit, I'd try to start speaking French and people would decide that their English was far better than my French, and would carry on in accented English. But now in the south-west of France, I was quickly realising this would be a very different experience entirely.

We weren't in a heavy tourist area like Nice or Provence. We were on the Atlantic side of the south and people spoke French. Period. Since we were so close to Spain, that seemed to be the second language, and after that, if you were lucky, you might find someone who spoke some English. I was in trouble. My doctor in Paris was American. Now we were in small-town France, and I had no doctor at all. And no house for that matter.

Breathe. Breathe. Breathe.

We were staying temporarily in a less than ideal apartment-hotel, and I was hell bent on getting out as fast as possible! There was no way I was going to bring my baby back to a place where I felt like I needed to wear flip flops in the shower.

We had seen a few options, which confirmed we'd be leaving our North American expectations at the gate of customs for this operation. We were in the small-town France now, and things were different: a little older, a little smaller, and generally just 'different'.

Kevin and I would exchange glances as the real estate agent brought us to house after house with weird quirks everywhere. One had a lone shower in the front entrance and another had the most horrid interior decor I'd ever seen. We weren't looking for a fixer-upper and we were going to be renting, which meant no redecorating. What we needed was something move-in ready, and the choices were looking slim.

Another house had a great yard that looked like a park, and lots of character as soon as we pulled up. When we went in we didn't know what to think. There were lots of little rooms with doors everywhere. One leading to the kitchen, another to the dining area and then one more to the living room. I felt like a kid in a fun-house. The house consisted of a tiny closet-size bathroom, the kitchen, with a stone oven like they have for pizza in Italian restaurants, the living room, dining area and a bedroom.

There's no basements in homes in France and with no staircase in sight, I shot a puzzled look to Kevin.

"*Y'a t-il plus de chambres?*" My funny look prompted Kev to ask if there were more bedrooms hiding somewhere since we only saw one.

"*Mais bien sûr.*" Of course there was and it was reassuring that the man showing us the houses made it seem like that was a crazy question. He could see by the state of me that we'd obviously be in need of more than one room.

He walked down the hallway, with us following closely behind him and about half way down he reached for a string that was hanging on a hook on the wall. With a swift pull of the string and an "*Attention!*" called out like a warning shot, a flight of stairs came down from the ceiling. He assured us that there was a lot more room up in the attic.

You've got to be kidding me.

Kevin humoured him and followed him up the creaky old stairs, but I was having nothing to do with those stairs because it would shatter my self-esteem if they broke under the weight of my pregnant body.

"Was it nice up there?" I sarcastically asked Kevin as he came climbing down, looking like a giant coming out of a doll's house.

"Ya, it was great. We could put your mom up there when she comes for a visit." Always a fan of the mother-in-law jokes, I smacked him on behalf of my mom.

This was clearly *not* the house!

Starting to get slightly discouraged, I hoped the last house had no strange quirks because I was now putting all my hope on it. We drove back to the edge of town and found ourselves in a little village that was just over a kilometre from the edge of Pau and from Kevin's office.

"This would be perfect. I could come home for lunch," Kevin said in disbelief. Going home for lunch was something he hadn't had the luxury of doing since elementary school. I hoped he wasn't going to expect daily grilled cheese sandwiches cut into triangles.

As we pulled into the driveway of the house, we were relieved that so far, there were no red flags. Nice yard, pleasant-looking house, average size. I liked the fact that there was an automatic gate at the end of the driveway. In Canada those were reserved for rich people with sprawling estates, but it would be weird if there wasn't one here. Not because everyone had massive properties with big houses, but because everyone had cement walls and gates marking out their property. Chalk it up to a French thing, but it was standard practice around these parts.

As we opened the doors we were greeted by panoramic windows boasting an incredible view of the Pyrenees Mountains. A quick glance to the right revealed an American-style, open concept kitchen, and I needed to look no further.

Without saying a word, I gave Kevin 'the eyes' that silently said: *I want this house.*

The house itself was modest by North American standards, with no basement and one simple living space. But by Parisian standards, the three bedroom, two and a half bath, with an open concept kitchen, was like winning the real estate lottery. Having lived my adult life in Western Canada, the idea of being greeted daily by a perfect view of the Pyrenees Mountains felt a bit like the Canadian Rockies, and it made my heart swell.

"Where do we sign up?" I said to Kevin, because the man who we actually needed to sign up with wouldn't understand what I said.

"Take it easy, let's just see the rest of the house first. We haven't even been upstairs yet." Always the rational one, that husband of mine.

I practised my patience and let the tour finish. But I knew we'd found our home. Our baby would not be born in a barn, but if they didn't let us in soon, he or she might be born in the dreary apartment-hotel we were staying in. The man told us we could get into the house in a month.

"But it's empty!" I nearly came flying out of my skin as Kevin squeezed my hand, holding me back from potentially hurting the man who didn't realise he'd just said fighting-words.

Trying to control my pregnancy rage, I faked calm and asked Kev to explain that there was a baby kicking at my ribs, ready to come out any time and there was no way I was going to stay in that depressing halfway house of a hotel for another month, waiting for my baby to arrive when this perfectly good house was sitting empty. I needed to nest, dammit!

Hell hath no fury like a heavily pregnant woman with nowhere to put her crib.

By the next week our names were brightly posted on the mailbox outside the gate and we were given our keys.

We had arrived.

Bringing Home the Bacon

With my nesting in full swing, we really started to feel like the house was becoming our home. We were also starting to realise that we were not used to the temperatures we were getting in the south of France.

It was August, and the mercury in the backyard was resting daily at thirty-eight degrees Celsius in the shade. The only thirty-eight degrees we were used to was the *minus* thirty-eight we'd get in winter back home. I remember once we ran out of ice cubes for drinks at a Christmas party and we just filled the tray, put it outside for a few minutes, *et voila,* instant ice cubes. Now here in *La France,* I was roasting in my own skin. I stalked around the house, closing the shutters on all the windows so the sun wouldn't come in and make the house hotter than it already was. I was pretty sure we could have fried an egg on our backyard patio tiles.

"Why is there no air conditioning in this country? How do these people survive?" I was not handling the heat well, and with the baby acting as a small furnace under my shirt, I was gripping the edges of sanity.

"Go sit in the car with the air conditioning on for a bit and cool off." Kevin threw me the keys, trying to be helpful.

"Great idea!" I tossed all care for the environment aside, went to the car and blasted the air-conditioning. Once all the vents were pointed directly at my sweating body, I snapped a picture of the temperature gage, immediately texting it to the ongoing 'family chat' conversation I had with my family back home.

"I'm sleeping," my brother pinged back.

Looks like the time change was blocking me from having anyone overseas keep me company while I cooled off in the car. After a couple of minutes I had convinced myself that the new neighbours were probably talking about me for recklessly polluting the earth with my car idling in the driveway.

'Just going to run to the store,' I texted Kevin inside the house. 'Ice cream will help.'

I had gotten used to driving a manual car, which was no easy feat! Now I was trying to master getting through roundabouts alive. Kevin didn't find it comforting that I would basically squeal the whole way through, and breathe a sigh of relief when I finally exited on the other side. But after a few lessons and some forced repetition, I was getting the hang of it.

Six roundabouts and three tubs of ice cream later, and I was back home, filling the freezer.

"I saw a sign at the end of the road. Something's going on in the village. We should go check it out."

Having nothing else on the agenda for the day, we made our way to the centre of our tiny little village, just outside Pau, where we were about to find out just how far from Paris we really were.

Each village throughout France has several things in common. They all have a *Mairie*, also known as city hall, a *Boulangerie*, to get your piping hot baguettes, *une église,* because France has churches everywhere and *une école* as village kids of course need to go to school. As the villages get bigger you'll find *un boucher*, to get your meat, *une pharmacie* for all your medicine, *un cordonierre*, to fix your shoes, and if you're lucky, *une pâtisserie*, to indulge in all your pastry needs.

Our new village had a church, a school, a little city hall and a bakery; just to give you an idea of its size. We were only a few minutes' drive to all the amenities we needed, but within our village things were pretty small and tight knit.

This was evident when the two foreigners rolled in.

"Everyone is looking at us," I whispered to Kevin as we walked over to the grassy area where the empty field had been transformed into a festival space, or *fête,* as the French say. It wasn't an enormous festival, but there were a few booths set up selling things and some other games going on a bit further along the field.

"You're just being paranoid." He took my hand and led us into the festivities.

I wasn't being paranoid, for once. People were totally staring at us. Kevin is what the French call *gusto.* He was a muscly two hundred and thirty pounds, standing tall at six foot two, which was basically a giant in France. I was so pregnant that a few more tubs of ice cream might have me rivalling Kevin's digits on the scale. Not to mention my hair had blonde highlights running through, which, thanks to the guy in Paris, I now knew was very un-French. And at five foot eight, I'm also quite tall myself. We might as well have been martians walking off a spaceship into this little village festival. People were *definitely* staring at us.

"Bonjour! Vous n'êtes pas d'ici?" We were greeted so typically with the standard, 'You're not from around here?' that seemed to be universal no matter what small town you walk into.

I wanted to shout out *'I told you!'* but nobody likes a know-it-all, so I made a mental note that I was right and carried on.

We explained that we were Canadian and we just moved to the village. Of course by, 'we explained' I mean Kevin. I let him do the talking because although my French was slowly coming along, big groups of people and a bit of a different accent was enough to throw me right off my game.

It didn't take long for word to spread that we were new in town. As we made our way through the festival, random people would walk by us saying, *"Bienvenue!"* I even had one person say, *"Wel-come"* to me very slowly and a little extra loud to enunciate their attempt at English. I guess word had also gotten out on my level of French.

"We have to play that game!" I announced as I pulled Kevin towards the most French festival game I'd ever seen. The beret toss.

Long measuring tapes were set up along the length of the field and contestants were given three berets. The concept was simple. Who could throw the beret the furthest? Seems easy enough, until you actually try to throw an empty beret any substantial distance.

My attempt was laughable, so no need to even go into any further detail, but Kevin, being of the athletic variety, really tossed that beret; getting a few *'Oh la laaaaa's'* out of the crowd.

"Tone it down there, big guy. You're drawing a crowd," I teased. But it was true. He looked around and his flushed cheeks gave away that he too was embarrassed by the unexpected attention.

"*Venez essayer celui-là,*" and without a further word of warning, he was being dragged by a local man, telling him to come and try out another game.

I scurried behind them, not wanting to miss a minute of Kevin being the centre of attention. They brought him to the station that had a Basque bowling game assembled. There were pins set up, just like in a bowling alley, but they were harder to knock over because they were made of solid wood. Instead of using a ball, they had wooden dumbbells that had to be tossed down the field to knock over the pins.

Dumbbells? Look out, village. Kevin was in his element. If you didn't know my husband, you might be quick to judge him as what some would call a 'gym-rat'. He loves lifting weights, and going to the gym is one of his favourite things to do. But he can't easily be classified as a weight-lifting junkie because he's also one of the smartest people I know. Kevin has a slightly photographic memory and the ability to randomly explain the history of the world, if pertinent to a conversation. You have to be careful what question you ask, because you might not have time for the answer. This leaves him resting comfortably in the 'intelligent gym-goer' category; however, I'm not sure this category is very common in France. In the south he regularly gets asked if he's a rugby player, and when he says, 'No, I work in geo-sciences,' people look at him like he has three heads. French scientists aren't known for lifting weights.

So, when I saw the dumbbells, I knew these French guys in their berets were about to get a bit of a show.

Kevin took a practice shot and the pins went down in one clean blow.

"*Jean-Marc, vien voir lui!*" Old men were calling their other old men friends over to see what was going on. After a few more throws of the dumbbells, it was turning into a bit of a spectacle.

There was a lot of chatter going back and forth in French, which I wasn't completely following, but I knew enough to tell that the old guys were excited.

Kevin turned to head back to me, clearly entertained by the excitement of the local men gathered around him, but as we were about to carry on to check out the last area of the festival, one of the men stopped him and told him that he couldn't leave because he was in the finals with Matthieu.

The finals for what, we didn't know yet, nor did we have any idea who Matthieu was, but these men were quite adamant about him sticking around.

"Are you tired?" Kevin asked, looking for an out. "We can go."

"And miss you in the centre of the action. Not a chance!" I was sticking around for this. I didn't care how hot it was or how badly I had to pee. It's not every day that your husband is in the finals of the Basque Games.

It turns out that Matthieu wasn't a local either; but he was a regular. His wife's parents lived in the village and they came every August and spent a few weeks in the region so his kids could spend time with their grandparents. Matthieu was about our age, making him one of the younger men in the crowd. He'd been the reigning champion of the local Basque Games for several years running, meaning that every year he took home the leg of ham.

Yes, ham.

My experience at fairs had me thinking we might win a big stuffed animal of some sort, but not at this *fête*. We were in the south of France and they loved their ham. The winner would take home an entire leg of cured meat, the kind you see hanging in the back of the butcher's shop. Before moving to France I referred to it in the Italian way, Prosciutto, but here in Basque Country it was called *jambon sec*. I had no idea what we would do with a giant leg of ham that was likely too heavy for me to even carry. It would be a lifetime worth of sandwiches and pork creations from Pinterest. But that stuff was expensive and all of a sudden I became an intensely competitive wife, *really* wanting Kevin to win. Second place was a case of wine, which was nothing to turn your nose up at, but we were in France, wine was cheap here. I had my sights set on the *jambon sec* and there was no turning back.

"I really don't care about the ham, Lis, we can go home and you can rest."

"Are you kidding me?" I took his face in my hands, looking him in the eyes with a seriousness he didn't often see. I was aiming for some kind of intense Rocky Balboa, eye-of-the-tiger vibe, but it probably came across a bit more, crazy-hungry-pregnant lady. "Win me that ham." I let go of his face and pushed him into the group of French men, ready for the action.

It was my first time at this festival, so I couldn't say for sure, but it seemed that the new foreign guy in town spicing up the competition for Matthieu was about the most exciting thing to happen around the village in a while.

It was go time.

Kev was introduced to Matthieu, shaking hands and exchanging a few pleasantries. I got myself a spot front row against the fence, in what seemed to be the wives' area. The men lined the sides of the 'alley' being ready to fetch the dumbbells and set the pins back up.

An announcer arrived, microphone in hand, voice echoing through the neighbourhood, drawing a crowd. He let everyone at the festival know that Matthieu had competition this year and *"Le Québécois"* looked ready for action.

Kevin wasn't from Quebec, but most people, especially in France, just assume that if you're from Canada and you speak French that you must be from Quebec. In my mind, he might as well be from there. He's from the edge of the province next door, where you could throw a stone and it would land there. The anglophone in me wants to paint that part of the country all with the same French paint brush, but look out if you have this conversation with Kevin because you may end up, as I've learned over the years, with a short history of the world, or of Canada anyway. Thankfully today was not the day, and he decided to let it slide, sending me a knowing look and amused smile that indeed he wasn't really *'Le Québécois'*.

"Bring home the bacon." I leaned over the fence and shouted to him across the field.

My humorous outburst was immediately followed by a small wave of shame and embarrassment. I forgot this was not a beer-league softball tournament, and people were suddenly staring at me. It's definitely not common to start shouting things out in English at a small-town French festival. And if it were, "Bring home the bacon" might not have been the classiest thing I could have yelled. Thankfully no one spoke English, but I immediately had all the ladies nearby battering me with questions in French. Most of the questions were confirming that I didn't, in fact, speak French.

"Non, je ne parle pas français mais j'apprends." I confirmed their suspicions, and told them I was learning.

Back at the dumbbell throw, things were getting tense. Kevin and Matthieu's scores were close, and I couldn't help but feel a bit bad for Matthieu. He was King of the village for years and assumed the title would be his once again. His mother-in-law was joking that she was expecting the ham, but her joke had a very serious undertone. Poor guys, the two of them were really getting the heat from the wives' section to win. The whole village was into this game, as if it was Game Seven of the Stanley Cup Finals.

And with one final toss of the dumbbell, I heard the announcer yell, *"Et le Québécois a gagné! Kevin est le nouveau champion!"*

He won! The leg of ham was ours!

Kevin and Matthieu shook hands, patted each other on the back, and seemed to have created a little friendship out there on the dumbbell field.

"Good job out there, slugger!" I winked as he came over, half-embarrassed, half-proud.

"Thanks," he smiled. "You all set to head home now?"

"Ya, let's go and get something to eat," I said as we walked towards the car, Kevin, with a lion's share of pork slung over his shoulder.

"How about a ham sandwich?"

Rolling with My Hommies

Having just gone through the friend-making process a year earlier, I knew what to expect. It would be hard work, a lot of effort, and it might be awhile before I even had anyone I could consider a friend. I was prepared for starting over, and hoping that there might be a few English speakers hiding around town; although from what I was seeing so far, that might be wishful thinking.

Kevin came home from work and let me know that he met a Scottish guy in his office whose wife ran a playgroup for English-speaking moms. He gave Kevin her number to pass along to me in case I needed, or wanted, to call her. That was all well and good, but I didn't even have a baby yet, so how was I supposed to show up at a playgroup without a kid?

With Kevin gone to work the next day, I puttered around the house and when that got boring, I sought out refuge from the heat by making an unnecessary trip to the frozen food aisle of the grocery store, again. Hanging out in one of the few air-conditioned buildings seemed to be my new favourite thing to do on those hot August days.

I started to get antsy late in the afternoon and decided it was time to take charge of my new life. I needed some friends. If I could do it once, as painful as it was, I could do it again. I knew it wasn't going to happen over night, and it's not like friends were going to come knocking on my door. I had to make it happen.

With a sigh, I walked over to the counter and picked up the piece of paper Kevin brought home from work the night before.

"Hi, Aurelie?" I wasn't sure I was even saying her name right. Apparently she was French, but was married to a Scottish guy and had lived in Scotland for a while. Hopefully her English was okay. "Your husband gave your number to my husband at work yesterday," I continued hesitantly, feeling a bit awkward calling a complete stranger.

"Lisa! I was hoping you'd call! Al said you might, and I'm so glad you did!" Her voice came through the phone; chipper, friendly and in impeccably perfect English.

I felt myself relax. After a brief chat she informed me that she had already let the other girls know that there was a new girl in town and they'd love to take me out for lunch the next day. She said she'd pick me up at noon and we hung up the phone.

There were other girls? And we were all going out for lunch tomorrow?

Well, that was much easier than I expected. I guess the new friends I was looking for were going to come knocking on my door after all. And it *was* going to happen over night. I couldn't be happier.

Aurelie arrived to pick me up right on time, if not a few minutes early. But I would soon come to know that right on time *was* a few minutes early for her and that was okay, because I no longer looked for a cookie cutter version of myself, or my friends back home, who were usually late like me. I quickly learned that Aurelie prided herself on punctuality and came to tease her about it in the years to come.

As we entered the restaurant, I saw a table of girls, all smiles, with piles of kids surrounding them. I loved kids, I was a teacher after all, but I just wasn't used to having them around in a social setting yet. My brothers both had kids, but obviously I didn't go out to restaurants with them very often since moving. My child was still sitting nice and quietly in my belly, so he or she was still quite easy to take care of. I was accustomed to long lunches involving wine; but lunches revolving around chasing toddlers through a restaurant was very new to me. My mom reassured me when I called her after lunch that babies don't arrive as toddlers.

"You have time to build up to that," she coached me. "They just poop and sleep for the first little while."

"Okay. I guess I can handle that."

Once I got acclimatised to the vibe of our lunch, it was clear that the girls were really nice. So much so, that I told them I could host playgroup at my house later in the week. They asked if I was sure, motioning at my giant belly, and I told them that I loved having people over and I didn't mind at all. It was true. I did love having people over. Mostly of the adult variety, since that was the only people I'd ever had over up until that point in my life.

A few days later, with company on its way, I made sure the house was clean and tidy, even though I absolutely hated cleaning and tidying. I didn't want my new friends to think I was a slob. With the house sparkling and fresh cookies were baking in the oven, I felt like a regular domestic goddess.

The doorbell rang at 9:23 and sure enough, it was Aurelie, right on time for the nine thirty start. I was happy that she was the first to arrive because then I was sure to know at least one person's name. Remembering names was always a challenge for me, especially when meeting a bunch of people at the same time.

Over the next half hour my front door let in a steady influx of English-speaking women from around the world and their children, anywhere from newborn to three years old. The place was packed and there were kids running everywhere. Actually, more accurately, there were kids eating, hopped up on cookies, covered in chocolate cake, and wiping their hands on my new couch, while running everywhere. It wouldn't be long before this scenario would seem perfectly normal to me, but in that moment, with my baby resting quietly and mess-free, in my belly, I thought those toddlers were crazy.

The women, however, were great. It was really hard to meet people in Paris, but maybe that's because I didn't have an 'in' with the mom-group women yet. Here in the second chapter of my France-life, I instantly had a house full of women, some with accents I struggled to understand, ready to add my number to their phone and make me their new BFF.

A few of the women stood out more than the others. One being Mary. She walked in and right away put out her hand to greet me.

"Hiya, I'm Ma-re. How ya goin?" she smiled.

"Marie?" I confirmed.

"No, love, Ma-re."

She seemed lovely, but I couldn't understand a word she was saying. Her accent was so thick that I struggled to even grasp her name. Aurelie came to my rescue. "Mary, you've met Lisa then?"

Ooooh, Mary. Why didn't she just say so?

I felt like she might as well have come up to me and said, 'Top of the mornin' to ya.' But that would have made her very Irish, and she wasn't Irish at all. She was Scottish, but I was new to the international scene and still getting my accents straight.

The third girl that stuck out in the group was Katrina. Hailing from Australia, with blonde hair and a cute little toddler trailing behind her, she seemed really nice. But it wasn't until everyone was leaving that I fell in friendship-love with her. As other moms were heading out the door, she went into my kitchen, grabbed the broom and started sweeping my floor.

"I'm not about to leave a pregnant woman with a mess like this," she said matter-of-factly as she fluttered around my house, picking up toys, clearing the table, and making right of my house again.

Within a heartbeat Mary and Aurelie had rallied around her and the chocolate cake disappeared from the floor and walls, couch cushions returned to their place and the landfill of juice boxes were tucked away neatly in the recycling bin. These girls were amazing. I'd known them for about half a second and they were acting like we'd been friends our whole lives.

"So what are your plans for the rest of the week?" they asked me.

"Ummm… no plans." I didn't want to come right out and say that they were the only people I knew here. But I didn't need to say it because they already knew and were changing that in a hurry.

"It's Natalie's leaving party tomorrow night. We know you don't know her, but it doesn't matter. All the girls are going out for dinner; it'll be a perfect time for you to meet everyone else. Can you be ready for eight?" They were all looking at me like they expected me to join them, even though I didn't know the girl whose going away party it was.

"I guess so…" I said, still unsure if I should crash the party, but focused on the fact that they said eight p.m. and not twenty hours. These were my people.

"Perfect!" Aurelie said with a smile. "I drive right by your house to get into town so I'll pick you up on my way."

And just like that, I had plans for the next night. Aurelie was coming to get me, and I'd be ready right on time, at 7:50.

Making friends in this town was nothing like I experienced in Paris. The year before I struggled to fall into a group of friends until I met my yoga girls because I just couldn't find where they were. Here in the south of France was a whole different story. The towns and villages were pretty small, but there were a few different companies in the area that were large enough to draw in expats. Since there was so little English spoken in the region, when these 'foreign' girls would meet each other, they would instantly become friends, as I was quickly finding out.

I arrived at dinner the next night and walked into a tiny restaurant that had been taken over by an international array of women. Many tables had been pushed together, creating one long line, with ethnicities rivalling a meeting at the United Nations. The common thread being, they all spoke at least a little bit of English. Some had older kids and knew each other from the International School, others had younger kids and were friends from playgroup, and some, like me, had just fallen into the group, and were welcomed wholeheartedly, no questions asked.

From that week on, I was never lacking for something to do, or someone to call. These girls were solid. I soon found out that most of their husbands worked with Kevin, and we were invited to picnics, BBQs and even the occasional hog roast.

This small-town living was just as you'd imagine what living in the French countryside would be like, right down to all the clichés of friends stopping by with warm baguette from the boulangerie. However, in my reality, that warm bread was accompanied by spicy curry, in hopes of getting that baby moving, because I was officially overdue.

A Manicure Like No Other

With the sweltering heat and me on the verge of exploding, the girls thought it might be nice for me to put my feet up and have a morning at the spa.

Kevin was happy to spend the morning golfing, so I set off on a girly morning of relaxation.

Picked up, of course, by Aurelie, I was starting to feel like I had my own personal driver. It was really convenient for me that she had to pass directly by my house in order to get into town, so she once again offered to pick me up. It was also handy that Aurelie's first language was French, although you'd never know it with her Scottish accent. She had called in advance and booked all of our spa treatments at the swankiest spa in town.

When Aurelie called to book the appointments, they confirmed that there was no pregnancy massage tables, so a massage for me was not an option. I could have chosen the mud wrap, but when you're full-term pregnant, and feeling big already, there's nothing appealing about being rolled in mud. So, I decided to get a manicure. If I was huge, at least I'd have nice nails.

Since there was a fairly big group of us meeting at the spa that morning, we had the entire place to ourselves. We felt like the 'Real Housewives of Small-town Southern France', even if it was just for that morning. We spent the next few hours bouncing between the jacuzzi, hammam, sauna, sitting in our spa robes nibbling croissants and taking turns going in for spa treatments. It was pampering at its finest!

When it came time for my manicure, I was dressed for the part in my crisp white spa robe and matching slippers. I followed the aesthetician into the treatment area, where we passed Mary, already set up at a manicure station getting her nails done. As I passed Mary, I flashed a quick smile in her direction, wondering how she was making out with her French small talk through that thick Scottish accent. As it turns out, Mary was fairly new too, and had just settled into this group of girlfriends a couple months ahead of me.

The woman brought me past my new friend at the manicure station, down a hallway, into a dimly lit room with a massage table. Clearly there'd been a mistake when booking my appointment.

"Je suis ici pour mes ongles." I told her that I was there to get my nails done. She confirmed that she knew and handed me a pair of disposable, see-through panties that they give you for massages, telling me to take off my bathing suit and put those on.

Was my French really that bad? She must not have understood me?

I repeated myself, *"Je suis ici pour mes ongles. Pour une manicure."* She again confirmed that she knew and told me to put on the little panties and that she'd be right back.

Left alone in the room, I had no idea what to do. If I was there for my nails, why did I need to get undressed? After all, I'd just walked by Mary, fully clothed, getting a perfectly normal manicure out front.

But the thing I'd come to learn about living in a foreign country and not being completely confident with the language, was that sometimes it was just easier to 'go with it' instead of asking questions.

So off came my bathing suit, and on went the tiny, disposable panties. They were incredibly small, obviously customised with the petite French woman in mind, and to be perfectly honest, I wasn't even sure which way the front was. Once again, this country had me feeling like an inadequate, awkward teenager. I was so confused by the situation I was in, and frustrated by the small panties that I threw them on, possibly backwards. Then I quickly put my robe back on because no sane person would stand there naked to get their nails done.

A moment later the woman came back and instructed me to take off my robe.

Now I was sure that we were having a language barrier. I tried one more time. *"Je suis ici pour mes ongles."* I paused for an extra second to make sure I had my vocabulary right, and I was positive that I told her, 'I'm here for my nails.' There should be no confusion.

But she was now clearly getting irritated with me, or maybe she thought that I was a slow learner, which technically, in French, it wasn't a stretch. With a sigh, she told me that she knew why I was there and instructed me to take off my robe and pass it to her.

Not wanting to irritate her further, I didn't fight it. I gave her my robe and stood facing her, totally confused, slightly embarrassed, and wearing nothing but the tiny see-through panties she gave me. I was starting to think that I might be on a hidden camera show.

I was then instructed to climb up on the massage table, and lay on my back. Totally exposed, thinking that this was insane, my eyes searched the room, looking for the hidden camera. This was way too weird to be real, someone had to be pulling a prank. But this is the nicest spa in town and there was no camera. It was just southern France, where nudity, apparently, wasn't really that big of a deal.

Eventually she covered me with a towel and did my entire manicure with me lying on the massage table.

When I made my way back to my friends, they greeted me with, "So, how was your manicure?"

"Naked," I said with a deadpan face. "I was completely naked."

Reading their faces was the quintessential moment of realising just how international my new friends were. I know you can't judge an entire country on one person alone, but in this case, that's exactly what I did. The expressions on the faces of the friends I had before me spoke volumes about the countries they came from. I had looks of shock, and giant question marks across the faces of those friends representing Scotland, Australia and the US. But then I glanced over at one of the girls from France, and in perfect representation of her country, she simultaneously raised her eyebrows, shrugged her shoulders and let out a blasé *'pfff'* sound, as if I just told her something as boring as, *'I had eggs for breakfast.'*

I never did find out why I was given a naked manicure and I likely never will. Maybe she didn't want me to have to stay in a wet bathing suit? Maybe she didn't feel like waiting for Mary's manicure to finish?

Whatever the case, this was how my life in France often was because I hadn't mastered the language yet. I'd find myself in strange situations that would never happen at home. Sometimes I could pull together the vocabulary to actually ask the questions I needed to, and other times, I just couldn't be bothered; and I'd find myself standing naked in a dark room with a strange woman, when all I wanted was to get my nails done.

Rejected

Nothing was open in Pau on Sundays. Paris was similar but with exceptions. Tourist areas would stay open, so if we were really bored, we could do touristy things, or go to those specific neighbourhoods and grab some mediocre food meant for non-Parisians.

Here in the south, we weren't in a tourist hot spot. Meaning, nothing was open and Sundays became a day to relax and hang around the house or outside. With the heat and my overdue pregnant belly, hanging around outside was not an option.

To clarify, I wasn't actually overdue. I was overdue by North American standards, where pregnancies are counted as forty weeks long. In France, they count forty-one weeks, adding one extraordinarily long week onto the end of pregnancy when you want nothing more than to meet your baby. So when I was told my French due date, I decided they were wrong. I would calculate the way 'my people' did: forty weeks. That day came and went, and I was still sweltering under the blazing French sun.

It was a crazy hot summer that wasn't letting up. Forty-two degrees Celsius with no air conditioning left me practically immobile. Going into the upstairs portion of our house, where our bedroom was, felt like an act of torture.

"I'm so hot and huge that it takes too much energy to transport my massive body around the house," I dramatically told Kevin, obviously looking for some attention.

We didn't want to drive to the ocean, even though it was only an hour away, because my overactive imagination had me conjuring up ideas of delivering the baby on the highway, or being closer to Spain than France and having to deliver the baby there, where not even my husband could help me with the language barrier.

"Let's go to the pool," Kevin suggested. "I know one that's actually open on Sundays."

And with that, we were out the door, and I was looking so forward to becoming weightless in the water.

This was the first time that I'd been to a public pool in France outside of the one that I used for knee rehab at our gym in Paris. Kevin was experiencing the French public pool system for the first time.

We walked in and searched for the change rooms.

"Where do we go?" he asked.

"I have no idea."

In Paris the pool was an extension of the gym, so there were separate ladies' and men's changing areas.

Not here.

Men and women had their lockers together and there were *'les cabins'* which were little changing stations in the middle, if you chose to use them. Then just before you got to the pool, it veered off in two separate directions when you hit the showers, but they were still fairly open concept. The unrestricted changing area was new to us, so we were a bit taken aback, but we were the foreigners after all, and the only ones who seemed at all concerned by the potential nudity. So, we went with it and made our way to the showers.

Rinsed off and ready to float, we walked through the little water area that cleans your feet and headed towards the pool when we were abruptly stopped by the lifeguard. He wasn't your standard Frenchman. This guy was big and he had a giant belly, which is the opposite of every French person I'd met up until this point, and every lifeguard I've ever met, for that matter.

"Je suis désolé, mais vous ne pouvez pas entrer." He told Kevin that he was sorry, but that he couldn't go in.

Judging by the pool full of people already swimming, the pool was clearly open.

"Pourquoi?" Kevin, totally confused, asked him why.

He told us that Kevin wasn't allowed in the pool because of what he was wearing. When we questioned what exactly the problem was with his outfit, the lifeguard suggested that his bathing suit was actually street clothes.

We were now totally confused. Kevin had no shirt on and was wearing bathing suit shorts. The kind that go to the knee; worn at the pool on vacation, for swimming, surfing and waterskiing. Kevin had worn a version of these shorts to swim every time he had been in water for his entire life. But this guy said he couldn't go into the pool with them. Completely puzzled, Kevin asked him what he was supposed to wear instead. We should have known.

A speedo.

Mr non-Baywatch Lifeguard told Kevin that there was no way he could let him in unless he was wearing a speedo. Kevin explained that I was obviously very pregnant and just wanted to float for twenty minutes. He promised that if he let us in, the next time we came he would buy a small French bathing suit. The lifeguard did not budge. He did, however, offer to lend Kevin his backup speedo that he kept in his locker.

We weren't sure how to respond to the lifeguard's generous offer of his spare speedo. Kevin composed himself and graciously declined, ensuring the world's strictest public pool security officer that next time he would surely come outfitted with the proper attire.

"Et un bonnet de bain aussi!" Mr Lifeguard chimed in.

"And a swim-cap?" I confirmed my French with Kevin, who nodded at me, even more puzzled by that than he was by the mandatory speedo.

We thought surely he was only referring to me with my long hair, but a quick scan of the pool confirmed that we were wrong. When, or should I say *if,* we were ever to return to the pool, Kevin would need to wear a speedo, and we would both need to wear bathing caps.

We weren't back home any more, that's for sure.

Where on earth had we moved?

Waiting on a Miracle

"Still no baby yet, I see," my mom joked as I came down the stairs in the morning.

"Nope. Not even a twitch." I slumped down on the couch, knowing later I would need to roll myself off in a very unsexy manner.

My mom had come from Canada to meet her new grandchild, but the baby had yet to make an appearance. Everyone was ready to meet *le bébé*, but he or she seemed to be quite comfortable inside my belly. Someone must have tipped my little French-fry off about the lack of air conditioning on the 'outside'.

"Let's go to Lourdes today," my mom suggested. "We might need a miracle if I want to meet my grandbaby before my flight home."

Lourdes was a Catholic pilgrimage site where the Virgin Mary was said to appear and over the years has become a huge religious tourist destination that happened to be only about twenty minutes from our front door. I have been known to refer to Lourdes as 'Vegas for Christians', because I was expecting a reserved, holy town, as if the whole place would be one big Sunday Mass. I was really caught off guard the first time I went there. The streets to get to the cathedral were lined on both sides with shop after shop of tourist trinkets, selling everything from sachets of lavender to life-size statues of the Virgin Mary. Restaurants had employees out front holding menus, trying to lure people in for lunch. The town had far more of a carnival feel than I expected from somewhere that was meant to be holy. But there was also a very high concentration of nuns roaming the streets, so whenever I visited, I kept my thoughts on the Vegas comparison to a minimum.

"I have another appointment with the doctor this morning to see what's going on in there. But if nothing's moving how about we go after lunch?"

"Sounds good to me," my mom replied, taking her coffee to her newly claimed spot on the back patio where she had a mountain view that would rival any observation deck of the Pyrenees Mountains.

"I guess I'll get myself ready and head out. Let me know if you need anything while I'm gone," and I did a ninja roll to get off the couch, with the grace of a hippopotamus.

When we moved from Paris, I was trying to quickly find a doctor. I wanted someone who spoke English, but what seemed to override that, was my intense, burning desire to have a natural birth. Having just finished my yoga teacher training, I was planning to use my months of studying *pranayama* to breathe my way through the delivery without so much as a grimace. I was zen, I was calm, and I was about to get the biggest reality check of my life.

Many of the new girls I'd met had their kids in Pau and encouraged me to go to their doctor because he spoke English. Most of the expats used him, but I was leery because when I asked the girls if he did natural births, I saw shifty eyes fill the room. Nonetheless, Kevin called to see if we could come and see the maternity ward and maybe take a tour since French hospitals, and how they worked, were new to us..

"Why would you want to do that?" he was asked curtly in French by the woman on the other end of the phone at the private clinic where the doctor worked. "We have an open house twice a year. If you want to tour through the clinic you will have to wait until October."

"I'm afraid we can't wait..." and before he could finish his sentence, she had bid him *au revoir*.

It was clear the French had a certain way of doing things, and bending over backwards for the non-French-speaking woman who was exploring her hippy lifestyle was not at the top of their priority list.

I'd gotten a lead on a hospital that was about twenty-five minutes down the highway, where they encouraged natural birth, and there was even a midwife that spoke English. I'm not talking about a French lady who took English in high school. This midwife was straight out of Ireland, and that, my friends, was the winning ticket.

We called the hospital and sure enough, I was able to come in for a visit, and they even looked at the schedule and made my appointment for a time during the shift of my Irish-saviour. How accommodating! If I wasn't at such a loss for words in French, I would have picked up the phone and given the other clinic a piece of my mind. But then I remember that wouldn't have been very 'zen' of me. The new Lisa just breathed her way through stress; so with a big exhale, I let it go and carried on.

Our visit to the down-the-highway hospital was encouraging. They supported my choice for a natural birth, although they did warn me that it would be difficult because it was my first baby and labour would be long. I told them that their hospital was where I wanted to give birth, and the drive down the highway with the speed limit at one hundred and thirty kilometres per hour would not be a problem.

Having gone through my entire pregnancy in France, I had been to many appointments at the '*gynécologie*', but it still caught me off guard at how things were done.

Nudity in a gyno's office in France was as normal as breathing. It just happens. Before moving to France, when I went to the gynecologist's office I was left alone in the room to undress and given either a gown to put on, or a sheet to cover up with. Then the doctor would gently knock on the door to see if it was okay to come in. The entire appointment was done while I was completely covered by a sheet or gown, without so much as a kneecap showing.

My doctor Paris had an 'undressing area' just beside the examining table where I could privately undress and hang up my clothes. Once my clothes were off, I was then expected to go and stand on the scale to be weighed. The problem being that the scale was clear across the room, far away from where they had me leave my pants and underwear. I'd say he was being a creep, but he didn't seem to even notice me pass by. The same rules applied if Kevin was there for the appointment. Everyone got a show. I always tried to remember to wear a long shirt on appointment days, but with my belly the size that it was, long shirts weren't so long any more.

As soon as I found my new doctor in the south of France, I quickly learned that the same 'no need to be shy' policy applied, but I was a regular now and checked my modesty at the door. I waddled myself over to the scale, terrified he was going to comment on my weight, or worse, say the number out loud. If I weighed more than Kevin I would curl up into a ball and cry. In all honesty I like to think that I wasn't actually *that* big for a full-term pregnant lady that was five foot eight. But compared to every petite French pregnant woman sitting in that waiting room, I was the Titanic.

"Don't even tell me," I told the doctor as he made his way past my half-naked body to the scale I was standing on. I was oblivious to the number as I could no longer even catch a glimpse of it hiding under my belly.

"You're okay," he said, but I think he just knew there was nothing I could do about it at this point. I was nearly crossing the finish line. That or he's seen pregnant women melt down before and he didn't want to go down that route. Either way, he was kind to me.

After I'd been weighed, I gave everyone a show again, under the unforgiving fluorescent lights, as I went over to the examining table and climbed up. Unlike my first appointment in France, I no longer waited for the modesty sheet. There wasn't much point in that after already prancing around the office naked from the waist down.

My checkup went well, and he assured me that it would be a miracle if the baby came today.

Hmmm. Maybe my mom was onto something with the Lourdes visit.

As I was gathering my things and the doctor and Kevin were discussing how busy the beaches down the road in Spain were, he added that there *might* be one way to get the baby moving if we were in a hurry, which we were because we didn't want to send my Mom home without some baby time.

"Ze Italian Induction," he tried in English for my benefit.

He explained to us what the French called the Italian Induction. In short: sexy-time.

This is just what every overdue pregnant woman the size of an elephant wants to hear when it's sweltering hot outside, you have no air conditioning in your house, and your mom is staying in the spare room.

"Ouff." I made a French noise just at the thought of doing 'it' in this heat.

"We'll see how Lourdes goes," I joked to Kevin on the way home.

Bonjour Bébé

We didn't get a miracle at Lourdes and we didn't get any lucky with the Italian Induction either. Time ticked on, and it turns out I was offering five-star accommodation on the inside, because our little French *bébé* had no desire to make an appearance. We were all getting anxious… especially my mom who had a flight back to Canada in a matter of days. My baby was fashionably late. How French!

I wish I could tell you that it all went down just as I imagined it in my head. That I painlessly gave birth to an angel in a field of wild lavender. Naively, that's pretty much what I was hoping for. All the yoga and meditating I'd done throughout my pregnancy left me pretty zen in my approach to the whole child birth situation, confident that I could breathe circles around any prenatal breathing class.

Oh, how I grossly underestimated reality. There was no lavender and the beautiful experience I was after ended up being a nightmare of epic proportions.

We got to the point where I would have to be induced, and what better time to do that than six a.m. on the morning of my thirty-first birthday. With the induction in full swing, I was still keeping to my plan of having a natural birth. It was going to be beautiful...

Until I found myself keeled over in the fetal position on the shower floor of the hospital room in sheer, crippling, knee-buckling pain. Things were getting serious.

"Looks like I'm going to be sharing my birthday from now on!" I tried to tell Kevin through gritted teeth. I was sure that we were nearing the finish line at this point. It was four p.m. in my mind, and sixteen hours on the French clock in the hospital. There was no way we wouldn't share a birthday now, I remember thinking.

The pain went from bad to worse and I was breathing my little heart out, pulling all the light and love from the universe that I could feel my yoga sisters sending me from Paris. I was still hanging in, and beaming proudly through the pain when the midwife complimented me on my stellar breathing skills. My Irish midwife was ironically nowhere in sight. Her being there was one of the factors that pushed me over the edge in deciding to give birth here and now she wasn't even in the building. She was on her four days off. At this rate I was wondering if I might still be here when she came back to work.

Hours passed and the pain continued to increase immensely. The induction had caused me to have intense contractions that were relentlessly close together, without making any progress on dilating. I was on a pain-train going nowhere!

After a midwife massaged my lower back with essential oils for far longer than she probably wanted to, I still found no relief. The contractions were rolling into one another and no amount of breathing could save me now!

"Let's try the tub," Kevin suggested with concern in his eyes.

I went into the tub and felt better for a few minutes. But the honeymoon was short-lived and the pain carried on fierce and hard! I went from in the tub to lying on the floor beside the tub without an ounce of grace or dignity left in my body. I couldn't find comfort.

Out of the tub, lying on the cold hard tiles wasn't working. Splashing around like Shamu the whale in the tub was also not a winner. I no longer wanted Kevin to touch me.

"You're doing amazing. But this is crazy, I think someone should check you," he suggested, on eggshells. Then, "I'll be right back. I'm just going to find a nurse."

With the shift change came a new nurse, quite concerned that my rolling contractions had been going on so long without any progress or pain relief. My birthday had come and gone, and to my shock and awe, there was still no sign of a baby.

"My wife wants a natural birth," my husband informed the new nurse and she looked over my chart.

"Screw that," I huffed. "This is f***ing INSANE! I WANT THE DRUGS!" I pleaded in English to a nurse that only spoke French.

Unsure how he should tread, Kevin double-checked with me about my decision. I was in too much pain to speak, but looked at him with eyes that were a mix of wounded puppy and serial killer.

"She's going to need some pain relief," he told the nurse.

They were talking in French and anything they said went right over my head, but in reality, at that point I stopped even trying to understand. Something was jabbed into my thigh. Things were a bit panicky. People were likely starting to become afraid of me, and there was no longer a trace of anyone who may have practised yoga in the room. I was cursing like a sailor and became enraged when I found out that the jab in the leg was actually going to *slow down* the contractions. Were they crazy? It had been twenty-four hours of torture and agony. I didn't want things to slow down. I wanted it to be over.

I demanded an epidural. I wanted relief and I wanted it now. I didn't give a damn about what it said on my birth plan. All the 'love and light' talk was a thing of the past. I wanted drugs!

Trying to stick as closely as possible to my initial wishes, they decided to give me an epidural, but just enough to provide some temporary relief. They offered me a low dose that would wear off so I could really, 'enjoy the experience' of the baby crowning and the actual delivery.

Hind sight is twenty-twenty.

I nodded, not really sure what I was agreeing to, but short-term relief was better than no relief at all.

With the pain subsiding, I was able to uncross my eyes and remember about that breathing business. My birthday was the day before and I took a moment to reflect that it was like no other I'd had before.

I was now thirty-one years old, and it turned out I wouldn't be sharing my birthday after all.

My first day as a thirty-one-year-old rolled on, and the epidural wore off.

I looked back at that stupid twenty-four-hour clock and I swore that I would not let it reach sixteen hours for the second time without this baby being born. I was getting close.

Fast and frightening, the pain was back, and I was on all fours, resembling a barn yard animal, but I couldn't care less. I'd do whatever it took to get the pain to lessen. I tried whatever they suggested but, once again, nothing was working.

I remember the last part in a blur... they said it was time to push. It was taking too long. My temperature was rising, or maybe it was the baby's? I made out the word forceps because it was similar to the English word. Some scissors entered the room. Naively, I wondered what those were for. Then the doctor had the forceps in hand, or was it the scissors first? I don't remember. All

I saw was the shape of the doctor's foot against the side of the table for leverage, and the table swaying slightly. I threw my head back in pain, exposing my tonsils, letting out subhuman sounds as if an exorcism was being performed. I left my body for a moment as I went into a place where the pain was beyond me. I was literally having an out-of-body experience. Scissors. Pain. Metal objects. I felt it all, as per the request on my stupid birth plan. It was beyond imaginable.

And then came love. Bigger and better than I ever could have imagined, kind of like the pain that preceded. The trauma that I was engulfed in moments earlier melted away as a little girl, screaming, just how her mother was seconds before, was placed on my chest. Love. All I felt was love.

With our new daughter safely placed in Kevin's arms, I went back to visit pain one more time, as what seemed to be a needle and thread came my way. Again, *au natural*. Bad idea. Quite possibly the worst I've ever had.

I'm sure Kevin still has nightmares of the sounds leaving my body in the delivery room. I'll tell you this much. That maternity clinic is no longer open. So that pretty much tells you everything you need to know about that slightly barbaric experience.

Searching for my lavender field childbirth may not have been the best plan I'd ever had, nor was the reality of it my finest hour. But at the end of the whole ordeal and once I came back to consciousness, I had the most beautiful little girl the world has ever seen. We called her Océane. Pronounced 'oh-say-an', it's a common French name and one of the loveliest names I'd ever heard. One of the Parisienne girls in my yoga training had a friend named Océane, and when I heard her name spoken for the first time, it may have been the pregnancy hormones, but it was like the heavens opened up and a choir of angels were singing. I ran home to tell Kevin that I knew what the baby's name would be if she were a girl.

He raised his eyebrows and said, "I really like it, but will your family be able to say it?"

As usual, he had a very valid point. It would take my non-French-speaking family some time, but they would eventually perfect their French accents.

Océane made it out in time to meet my mom. All that time I spent in the hospital gave my mom a chance to fill my freezer before she flew back over the pond, and I wasn't too proud to stop her!

It was a frenzy of excitement. When my mom left, Kevin's mom arrived. The girls were stopping by to meet the baby and drop off gifts and food. In France you have three days to legally declare your child's name to the *Mairie.* I suppose that's how Océane's birth announcement ended up in the local paper, because it wasn't us who did it. That's likely what tipped off the mayor, who popped by the house with a bouquet of flowers when I got home. Small-town living at its finest.

So there we were, three peas in a pod: Kevin, myself, and our sweet little Océane who cried all the live long day.

I knew babies cried, but I assumed they stopped at some point. We fed her, changed her, walked her, sang, danced, drove her around in the car, held her while we gently bounced up and down on a fitness ball. We didn't know a lot about babies, but we did know that ours cried *a lot*.

For three months to be exact. It didn't matter how many parenting books I bought online, or how many check-ups at the doctor we had, she loved to cry. We heard all sorts of terms like reflux and colic and French words that I didn't understand. I was sleeping in forty-five-minute increments for months and between the exhaustion and the French, the pediatrician's medical jargon was flying right over my head. Thankfully, Kevin was taller than me, catching everything that flew over my head, saving the day with his perfect French, being able to make sure there wasn't something seriously wrong with our opera-singing baby.

And so we did the best we could, while she 'sang'.

Reunited

Crying or no crying, it was Christmas and we had already booked out tickets home, so we were going to have to figure it out. Actually we had already booked *my* ticket home, so it was all on me. Kevin had to go to Paris for two weeks to finish up his master's degree and present his thesis. He had a hotel around the corner from the Eiffel Tower where Océane and I would be joining him for the first week, then the two of us would fly to Canada, get some extra visiting in and Kevin would join us a week later when he was done.

The week in Paris was wonderful. In some ways it felt like everything was the same and no time had passed; yet in others, the new member of our family had made it seem like the whole world had changed.

This time in Paris gave us a chance to see some of the adjustments we'd be making had we decided to stay. Good news was we hadn't had any kids before this, so we didn't know that the challenges we faced in the city weren't necessarily 'normal'. Plus, we loved Paris, so we just made do.

A few of the biggest struggles were getting on and off the Metro. The first few days I tried to bring the *pussette.* Even though we bought the stroller in France and it was fairly small, we couldn't get it throughout the turnstile to get into the Metro. Sometimes there were wheelchair access points, others there weren't. The Metro was generally not wheelchair or stroller friendly. There are always stairs, and even though people are normally quite quick to offer to lift the front of your stroller down the stairs, it was a real pain to transport it. After two days Océane was on a baby-carrier-only transportation system.

This worked great for walking around town, and for riding the Metro, but it sucked when I wanted to stop in a cafe, or restaurant, because instead of having my sweet baby sleeping, hanging out in her stroller, she was attached to me at all times. Odds were high she was going to get *creme brûlée* dropped on her head at some point over the course of the week.

But her not having a stroller to sit in for the long-drawn-out meals we were used to in Paris, was not a problem on this visit. We quickly found out that our little crier was going to be cutting our meals short. We had a few dirty looks from grumpy waiters, eyeballing our direction and telling us to *'make the crying stop'* with their eyes.

Trust me, buddy, I would if I could.

I was also happy to bolt from the restaurants because I was worried about whipping my boob out to breastfeed. I was still new at being a human milk dispenser, and the restaurant tables were so close together that I might as well have been breastfeeding while sitting on the lap of the man beside me.

"Maybe I'll just go see if there's a chair outside the bathroom or something," I whispered awkwardly to Kevin as we were having lunch with some of his friends from grad school. These were friends that were a bit younger than us, had no kids, and typically didn't have their buddy's wife showing her boobs mid-meal.

This breastfeeding-in-public-business was tricky.

I went down the tiny winding staircase to try and find a quiet spot to expose myself, but I knew Paris, and deep down I knew that I'd be out of luck before I even looked. Space was at a premium in these places. You could barely turn sideways in the toilet, and the sink area was so small that there's nowhere to put your tiny purse, never mind diaper bag.

I wasn't sure how I was going to pull this off. Océane needed to be fed and changed, and my options were to do so at the table in the packed restaurant upstairs, which is likely uncomfortable for young French guys at our table. Feeding her, okay, but changing a stinky diaper at the table where other people are eating is just not cool. Option two would be to try and find somewhere downstairs to do it. Or option three, to somehow magically do it all while standing up.

It looked like option two was my only real choice. The space in the bathroom area was the size of a large refrigerator box. There was no chair. There wasn't even any empty space on the ground besides the area you stand when you wash your hands. Bathrooms in Paris cafés are all function, no fashion. Space is a luxury that Paris bathrooms usually didn't offer. So, I was left with a toilet that was nearly touching the sink and not much more space than that.

I opened the door to the space that housed the toilet, and hung my bag up on the back of the door. It was a pleasant surprise to actually find a hook. Trying my best to not make contact with the toilet seat, I used my elbow to put down the lid as I set up shop. I hoped no one was going to need the bathroom for the next twenty minutes because I was serving up a gourmet meal in there.

When the milk connoisseur had had her fill I was onto challenge number two. Literally.

How was I going to change her diaper in here?

This was not time to let my inner germaphobe come out. Without overthinking it, I pushed down my fear of all things grotesque and summoned my inner Mamabear to take over. It was a new role, but I was figuring it out.

I grabbed my change mat and laid in on the lid of the small Parisian toilet seat and tried not to think about all the tiny French bums that passed through this area. But they really were tiny bums because the lid was so small that Océane, at eight weeks old, could barely fit when I lay her down. I balanced her with one hand, having deadly visions of her wiggling off onto the *dégueulasse*, disgusting floor. I heard someone trying the door handle which was only adding to the stress of trying to clean up the messy newborn diaper.

"*Désole!*" I shouted an apology to the person trying to get into the bathroom.

When I finally exited the tiny space, and he saw me with a baby, and the bag of stuff that comes with leaving your house with a newborn, he gave me a warm, empathetic smile and replied that it was okay, *"C'est pas grave."*

See, Parisians weren't so bad.

By the end of the ordeal I was sweating and slightly overwhelmed, but Océane was fed and changed without having to do it on top of the table in the overcrowded restaurant.

Those were the challenges of Paris with a newborn. On the upside, we were back in Paris, our former home. The city of lights. There's a magic about Paris that you can't find anywhere else in the world. And even though I had to change my new baby on the back side of a toilet seat and hoped that the food came quickly before she started crying whenever we were in a restaurant, I was happy we were there.

I met up with my yoga girls and showed them their yoga-baby that they'd been singing to and rubbing through my belly for the seven zen-filled months. We visited the Christmas markets and roamed the cobblestone streets, as a party of three, instead of two.

After being strapped to my chest for a week, it was Océane's new favourite place to be. We said goodbye to Kevin and Paris, I put on my cutest new eight-pound accessory and pushed an empty stroller through the airport. If I could navigate my way through a week of living in a Parisian hotel with a colicky eight-week-old, I could sit on a plane for eight hours. The best part: there was a change table on the airplane so I'd be going back to a more civilised way of changing my baby. Strangely, compared to the stuff I was pulling as a tourist trying to change diapers in Paris, I honestly thought that the airplane change table was pretty luxurious in comparison... until I got back to Canada.

"Wanna go to the mall?" my cousin Alyssa asked me over the phone a couple of days after I arrived.

Alyssa and I had our first babies one day apart, so we were pregnancy buddies all the way through. We even had an international texting frenzy when she went into labour and I followed not far behind with labour pains of my own.

Of course I wanted to go to the mall. It was December in Canada and I was freezing cold. The mall had underground parking, so from the attached garage at my parents' house to leaving my car and going into the mall meant that I wouldn't even need to have the frigid subzero air touch my skin.

As we started shopping we headed straight for a coffee, and I couldn't help but take in my surroundings. It was a sea of stroller-pushing, yoga-pant-wearing moms with to-go cups. And that's when I noticed what

I was lacking. All these Canadian moms had SUV-style strollers. They were rolling in style and I was jealous.

"Here, give me your jacket," Alyssa said, putting my jacket, her jacket and both of our diaper bags under her stroller.

Was this some kind of sick joke? I could barely fit a package of wipes under my Euro Stroller.

Alyssa reached out her hand. "I'll take your tea too." And she slid my to-go cup into one of the three cup holders on her Cadillac of strollers. Our vehicle in France didn't even have a cup holder, and her stroller had three. I was officially a foreigner in my own country. I was pushing a Smart Car in the land of SUVs, and from what I saw when we went through a baby store later on, I'd purchased half the stroller for twice the price. Lucky me.

It didn't take very long to get over my stroller envy, but I quickly turned green again when it was time to feed our babies. There was no turning down toilet seats at this mall. Alyssa led me into the 'nursing lounge' and my mind was blown. I'm sure these places existed when I lived in Canada, but I was nowhere near having kids so clearly was oblivious.

We opened a door to a room that was outfitted with eight swivelling leather lounge chairs, each accompanied by its own side table, should you need to rest down a bottle or cloth. There was a huge TV mounted on the wall, an area in the corner for toddlers to play, microwaves, two changing stations, sinks, and bottle warmers. I was just waiting for a magician to pull a rabbit out of a hat. This place was unbelievable. It couldn't be more different from what I had just experienced in Paris if I dreamed it up myself!

As I got back into my car to drive home, I was still in shock by the contrast between my old 'home' and my new one. France was wonderful for so many reasons, as was Canada; and the differences couldn't have been displayed better than in that mall bathroom.

Before I started to drive back home, I called Kevin so I could catch him before the time change worked against us.

"What are you up to?" I asked.

"I was just about to go for a stroll and grab a bite to eat. I forgot how nice Paris is at night." I could tell he started walking as he talked to me. "How about you? What are my girls up to?"

"You'll never guess what I just saw." And I told him all about how I just left the twilight zone.

The Vagina Games

Our trip to Canada was amazing, and we showed off Océane as if she was a gold medal from the Olympics. But by the end we were tired, and ready to get back to our normal routine. To go home, after visiting home is a strange thing, but France definitely felt like where we belonged now, especially with our new little addition.

Yes, she still cried a lot, and that probably made the people around us on our flight slightly irritated. But they got over it, because there was no other option, nor did we.

Then one miraculous day, out of the blue, without anything changing, as if by magic, the three months of crying ended. The heavens opened up, birds were singing, our ears stopped ringing and we had come out of the colic-cloud. We weren't sure if the crying would ever end, but when it did we couldn't have been happier.

You'd think that after coming out on the other side of three months of house bound crying that I might have somewhere exciting to go. Maybe to run some errands, go shopping, visit some friends? I did none of those things.

Instead I headed to my friendly neighbourhood midwife, as requested by my gynaecologist. I had been to my six-week checkup the month before and was written a clean bill of health. My doctor gave me a slip saying that I needed to do the standard ten sessions with the midwife that all French women did after child birth. Unsure what to expect, I chalked it up to a 'when in France' moment and made the appointment once things had settled down and I could comfortably leave the house without my child sounding like she was being kidnapped.

Océane and I sat patiently in the waiting room, her in her bucket car seat, while I flipped through French magazines, letting the words blur in front of my eyes. There was a time where I would have tried to actually read the magazine and practise my French, but that day I was just happy to just look at the pictures.

I had no idea what to expect from this appointment, but if it's a standard set of appointments that all French women do after child birth, how bad could it be. *Right?*

When I was called into the office, I placed Océane in a baby swing that they had set up in the corner. Clearly they knew their clientele. She was happily swinging away to the sounds of lullabies, and I was invited to have a seat at the *sage femme's* desk so we could start my file. It was serious business at the midwifery's office.

Had I known these questions she was going to ask me would be so embarrassing, I would have put a little foundation makeup on to cover up how much I was blushing. But I had no way of knowing, so instead I just stared at her in disbelief and muttered out the best answers I could manage as she fired away at me with some intensely personal questions.

Do you pee when you sneeze? Can you have a shower without peeing? How is your sex life? Can you feel your husband inside you?

Did she really need to know all this, or was she just curious? I couldn't believe that these were her standard set of questions. If that was her way of easing into things, I was getting a bit nervous to find out where the rest of the appointment would take me.

After our little Q&A session, she led me to the examining table where she informed me that she would be giving me a quick internal exam.

The fun just didn't end.

I wasn't thrilled to have to get an internal exam, but after just having given birth at 'Hippies r Us', I had no modesty left. I got up on the table and let her do her thing.

Initially I did my standard stare-at-the-ceiling routine, but then she started asking me questions. Not your typical 'Are you okay?' questions either. She was asking me about upcoming holidays, what my plans for the weekend were. This was no quick internal exam. She was camping out in there, having me contract and relax for ten seconds at a time, all the while making polite chit chat as if her fingers weren't resting comfortably inside of me. *What the hell was going on?*

The French called this set of appointments, *rééducation du périnée*. Perineal reeducation, and much to my disbelief, I was just getting started.

Next I was given my very own reeducation 'tool' to keep (thank God we didn't have to share). She called it a *sonde*. It was a wand that resembled a mini-zucchini, or a large hot dog, maybe a small banana. I'll let you use your imagination.

After a lot of contracting, relaxing and talking about my weekend, I finally had my personal space back, but I was instructed to put the *sonde* inside myself.

It had a cord on the end that got plugged into her computer and I couldn't help but feel like this was going to end badly. I followed instructions like the good little confused foreigner that I was, and waited as she turned on the computer. The screen came to life and I was thrust (pardon the pun) into a gamer's paradise. That's right, I was going to play video games with my vagina. This was an insane situation to find myself in considering that I had no idea what to expect from the appointment. On the screen I was represented by a yellow dot. The aim was to keep my yellow dot between the lines as it moved along the screen, controlling the movement by contracting and releasing on the wand inside of me, all the while receiving light electric shocks from the wand that was simultaneously strengthening my pelvic floor. I couldn't quite believe that I was willingly electrocuting my lady parts.

I needed to get home and tell Kevin about what had happened. But being a natural over-sharer, I told Kevin, along with everyone else I knew, because I just couldn't believe that this was common practice in France.

Once I got over the initial shock factor, I warmed up to the idea. I liked knowing that I was part of the secret, French, 'don't mess with my strong vagina' club. Maybe I was the only one that thought it was crazy, but how great that the French government wanted their women to have bad-ass pelvic floors that could withstand trampolines, sneezes and banish the need for panty liners while running. I embraced the pink-part video games and was going for high score. I had nine more rounds to firm my position.

By my last session, I was a seasoned pro. The internal exam no longer even fazed me and I brought in the recipe for the 'American style' cookies I brought the midwife the week before (also known as chocolate chip cookies). We were becoming like besties and the fact that nine appointments ago being there was the weirdest thing I'd ever done, seemed a little less weird now.

I saddled up with my joystick like a true French woman, and I couldn't help but feel a bit like an Olympian training for the Vagina Olympics. The midwife was at the computer, turning up the level of electric shock coming through the wand, waiting for me to give her the *okay*. She started looking at me strangely as I told her I still felt nothing and that she could put the shock-level higher. Hesitantly, she cranked the voltage a bit higher, and then higher some more.

"I must have the world's strongest vagina?" I said with a smile. However my humour was lost in translation, and she just gave me an awkward smile. She told me that it's strange I couldn't feel anything because it was on a very high setting and that she better not put it any higher. Clearly I was ready to win the gold medal in reeducation. I shifted ever so slightly on the table to make a kissy face at Océane in the baby swing and that's when without a flicker of warning, I released a subhuman sound that I'm sure could have been heard at the top of the Eiffel Tower. I was jolted into a star fish position on the examining table and was paralysed with fear at the thought of moving a muscle.

Apparently my gold medal vagina just had the *sonde* in on a bad angle. The midwife dove for the off-switch and came to my rescue before I scared away her other clients in the waiting room.

When I got home that night, Kevin actually asked me why I was walking funny, and when I told him the drama that unfolded at the midwife's office, he looked at me with disbelief painted all across his face.

"Believe it, babe," I told him with a sigh. "It's tough being a French woman."

Is There Corn in My Teeth?

Kevin's new 'work wife' was lovely. She was around our age, but started having kids earlier, so she'd been through the newborn stage already. She helped Kevin ease into parenthood with the wisdom of a French mother when he would arrive to work with bags under his eyes from not sleeping.

After they'd been working together for a while, we decided we'd have her and her husband over for dinner. The problem with inviting French people over to your house for dinner is that they're used to things being done a certain way. It can be a bit stressful to make sure you've got things just right.

I hoped I was well enough prepared. We were going to stick to a few of the French standards; I had the Champagne chilling for our *aperitif,* fresh baguette to be served with dinner, and a cheese platter was ready with giant chunks of the stinkiest cheese I could find, ready to be served *after* dinner, but *before* dessert. There was just so much to remember.

Anne-Marie, Kevin's colleague, always thought it was funny that us Canadians BBQed all year round; but there was no reason not to, because winter here was like fall where we came from. It was perfectly acceptable in our books to keep the grill going year round. I assumed I would make some kind of dinner party etiquette *faux pas* by French standards, so I decided to cover my bases by inviting them for a 'Canadian style' BBQ. That way, when I dropped the ball on something, like not having the table formally set with stemware and cutlery everywhere, I could just say it was the relaxed Canadian BBQ theme. I thought it was a great idea, and I also didn't have to wrack my brain too much thinking of what to serve. Casual BBQ: I could do that with my eyes closed.

Our guests arrived, and my knowledge of French manners were put to the test right away. We started with *les bises,* and kisses were flying everywhere. Kevin kissed Anne-Marie once on each cheek as she walked in, and I followed behind him. He shook her husband's hand, even though you will see French men *fait la bises,* he decided not to dude-kiss. I knew enough that the hand shake wasn't the right choice for me. I went in for the double kiss, but clearly fumbled and went for the wrong side first which left us nearly kissing on the mouth. Trying to rectify the situation, he went the other way, but so did I at the same time. This couldn't get any more awkward if I tried. I laughed it off and eventually, although not painlessly, the kisses were delivered.

Next up on the set of awkward formalities: the *tu vs vous*.

In French *vous* refers to a group of people. But that would leave things far too simple; so the French also use *vous* as the polite form of 'you'. This form of vous is meant to be used out of respect in a formal setting like work, if you are speaking to someone older than you, or if you are meeting someone for the first time, as I was with Anne-Marie's husband. But I was always getting my *tu* and *vous* mixed up. When Kevin and I would (rarely) practise French, I would 'vous' him and he'd laugh, telling me I didn't need to 'vous' my own husband. But when it was time to 'vous' someone, like a delivery man, or neighbours I didn't know well, sure enough, 'tu' came out.

Tonight was no different.

"*Bonne soirée. Ca va?*"

"*Oui, ca va et vous?*" I said to Mr Anne-Marie, then realising maybe I should *tu* him because we're all supposed to be friends, I quickly tried to rectify myself, not wanting him to think that I thought he was old and stuffy. I shook my head. "*Tu. Tu va bien? Ou vous? Désolé.*"

This was getting more awkward by the minute with me apologising for stumbling over my words. Time to open the Champagne. That always helped.

What casual BBQ doesn't start with Champagne, right? I was pouring with a heavy hand, hoping social lubricant would help get me through my first real dinner party with French guests and not mess it up any more than I did in the first few moments that they walked in. There was a fine balance between a couple of glasses of bubbly to settle the nerves, and a couple *too many* glasses of bubbly, leaving you no longer interested in serving your guests dinner. Thankfully when it came to this, I was a tightrope walker; and with many years of practice, that was one line I had perfected walking... usually.

I quickly forgot about my blunder at the front entrance, and was now fluttering around the house giddy on Champagne bubbles. I refilled glasses and passed out napkins for the cocktail nibbles, like the perfect hostess. As usual, once I got a couple of drinks in me, my French got better with every word I uttered. Kevin smiled, half because he loved hearing me speak French and half because he knew the Champagne was taking effect. The bubbles had gone to my head and any nerves that were once lingering were now nowhere in sight. There's something to be said for letting go of your inhibitions.

I'd prepared most of our meal ahead of time because nobody likes inviting guests over and then spending all night in the kitchen. We'd be having salad, roasted potatoes, green beans, corn on the cob and Kevin would grill steaks. Cooked rare, of course, because there's no other way for the French to consider eating a steak.

When we first arrived in France, I was a medium-rare kinda girl. But as the years rolled on, the French had worn me down, and I liked my steak as rare as the next French guy. Basically most people *en France* just like their steaks warmed up on each side. It makes for quick grilling anyway.

With the meat off the grill in record time, we gathered around the very casually thrown together table, where I played the Canadian BBQ card, mainly because many years of catering banquets through university has caused me to hate setting the table. As much as I love it when I sit down at an elegant table, that elegant table usually never appeared at my house.

"Make yourself at home, this is really casual." I can hear my mom's voice echoing in my head as the words come out of my mouth. That is, *if* my mom spoke French of course; because by Champagne flute number three, (*or was it four*) I had completely switched over to French, no longer caring when I fumbled my grammar.

Red wine splashed into our oversized glasses (again, very unFrench... the extra large stemware, not the wine) and we touched glasses, "*Santé!*" To your health, making eye contact as we did cheers, because it's considered bad luck not to lock eyes with the person you're cheering.

"*Bon appetite!*"

And with that, we all daintily began eating with our forks facing down. This is also something that I had to learn over time once moving to France. I consider myself to be well-mannered, but until crossing the pond, both Kevin and I ate fork up. One day Kevin came home from work, where every day he eats with French people, and asked if I had noticed that everyone ate with their forks facing down. It was true. Food delicately balances on the back side of the fork whenever I've checked since. To me it defeats the purpose of the curve in the fork, but I don't want to look like I have poor table manners, so ever since Kevin pointed it out, we've both taken note, turned over our forks and stopped switching the knife back and forth every time we had something to cut. The French didn't mess around with switching; the knife stayed in the right hand, and they managed to just eat with their fork (turned under) in the left hand. You practically needed a degree to keep up with all these unwritten social rules. And we were about to learn a few more!

Without meaning to, Kevin and I had coincidentally both left our corn untouched until later in the meal. Kevin caught our dinner guests exchange a quick confused glance, like they weren't sure what to do with what was on their plates. He immediately caught on, and realised that for some reason, they had no idea what to do with the corn on the cob. I had cut them in half to make them more manageable, but it didn't even cross my mind to think that French people don't eat anything with their hands. There's no chicken wings, mozzarella sticks or nachos on menus here. Anything you ever eat is done with your fork and knife.

Not at this BBQ.

Kevin jumped in as soon as he noticed and led by example, picking up the corn and biting into it, turning it as he went, like we both grew up doing. A brief look of relief flickered across the faces of our guests and quickly they followed suit, picking up their corn, just as Kevin had. There we were, like a bunch of beavers, gnawing away at our corn on the cob, perfectly normal for Kev and I, but not so much for our guests.

I never thought that there was anything wrong with eating corn on the cob until this incident caused me to analyse it. I guess it is a little barbaric, not to mention that you usually spray your neighbour with flying corn juice: all, once again, very unFrench. It's just not something French people tend to eat. Which explains why corn in a can is readily available, but trying to buy corn on the cob is quite challenging. I only know of one store that sells it, and for the price of two ears of corn I could have bought several cans of corn. Now I know why: it's probably specially imported for me, the only one buying it.

Our guests were kind and didn't seem to mind, once they knew what to do with the food on their plate. Do we still eat corn on the cob at our house? Absolutely. Do we still serve corn to French people when we have dinner parties? Absolutely not.

Running Away from Home

The flurry of carbohydrates from fresh bread products and pastries that crossed my lips throughout my pregnancy may have had something to do with why I gained more weight than your typical French woman, who stereotypically practised some sort of restraint. Of course they could refrain from eating everything they saw, they grew up with the stuff within their grasp at a moment's notice. I, however, did not find these heavenly shops littered throughout my neighbourhood. It's a blessing and a curse really.

I'm going to stick with saying that fifty pounds (or twenty-two kilo because it sounds like less) was the amount of weight I gained during my pregnancy. However, when I neared the end of my pregnancy, and saw numbers being displayed on the scale, I made a personal decision to stop looking, so perhaps it might have been a bit more than fifty pounds. Or less! You never know, right?

Being the young naive woman that I was, I assumed that baby weight would just fall off... or out. *Maybe that's what after birth was?*

You can imagine my great surprise when my sweet baby was born, and all 8.4 pounds of her were no longer attached to me.

I can round up and count the actual 'baby weight' as ten pounds, plus an extra five for water and whatever else was floating around in there. That means that after I was no longer pregnant, I was still carrying an extra thirty-five pounds of indulgence attached to my midsection and thighs. This was not good.

Spring arrives early in the south of France, and there wasn't a chance that I would be caught dead wearing my maternity shorts because my regular shorts still didn't fit. That was not the look I was going for. Action needed to be taken, and I knew who the man to whip me into the shape was, even if I was feeling too lazy to put in the work it would take to get there.

"Keeeeeeeev," I whimpered in the best 'please help me' tone I could muster up. "I don't want to wear parachute panties any more."

"What's wrong with your granny panties?" He tried to hold back his smirk.

"They're disgusting. I need you to help me lose weight."

"Sure. You want to go out to the garage and lift some weights while Océane is still napping?"

We had a full gym set up in the garage that was attached to our house. The French aren't big into gyms because it's just not part of their culture. Especially in the slow, relaxed pace of life in the south. But it was part of our culture, and a big part of Kevin's favourite pastime, so he decided to order weights for a home gym. About five hundred pounds worth of weights to be exact. You can imagine the poor delivery guy who was stuck dropping off this package while Kevin was at work. It wasn't unusual for our garage door to be open and have the neighbours walking by while Kevin was squatting three hundred pounds in the garage. We're definitely known as the weird foreigners in the neighbourhood.

"No, I don't want to lift weights. I think I want to start running again, but I don't actually *want* to run. I just want to fit in my clothes."

I was dreading the thought of it! No one likes doing something they suck at, and there was no denying that after such a long hiatus from my running shoes, I would most definitely suck. But I wanted my regular panties back, not the ones that were big enough to cover the hole in the ozone layer; so run I must.

I couldn't help but think back to when we first arrived in Paris, before I buggered up my knee. After leaving everything behind and landing on a new continent, I needed something to keep me busy, challenge me and clear my head.

Running was my friend in a country where I didn't yet have any. I started signing up for races and actually became quite a good runner. I wasn't Forrest Gump, but I could crank out twenty kilometres, barely breaking a sweat.

My last running memory I was flying through Paris, uber fit, feeling like a machine. Now all I felt were the seams of my running pants holding on for dear life as I pulled them up over my unexercised thighs.

"You have to start somewhere," Kevin encouraged me. "Just take it slow and see how far you can go."

I dug to the back of my closet, and found my running shoes. How could something that was once my favourite thing look so foreign and unappealing? It felt like I opened up my high school yearbook and was looking at a picture of my first boyfriend. *Really? We were an item? We had a spark?* I couldn't even imagine it any more. My running shoes, like a photo of my first boyfriend, were not igniting any internal desires.

Kevin, being one of those annoyingly 'naturally athletic' people, could see I was defeated before I even started. He walked over to the shoe closet, picked me up from the pool of sadness I was swimming in and grabbed me by my shoulders for a pep talk.

"I'm proud of you for wanting to get out there. Give it your best shot. Even if you can only make it couple kilometres; it'll get easier next time."

He was right. I might not be able to whip off five kilometres in my first trip back outside, but it was better than hanging on the couch eating Ben & Jerry's. Better for my waist line anyway.

I laced up, dramatically taking a Usain Bolt stance in the front entrance to get a laugh out of Kevin, and I was off!

I made it just past the mailbox before I needed to stop and catch my breath. I didn't know whether to laugh or cry.

He could have set the bar lower on his pep talk! He had me thinking I might be able to pull off a couple of kilometres, and I could barely run thirty seconds. How depressing. I ended up running 1.25 kilometres in total and I must have stopped nine times because it felt like there was an army of angry dragons breathing fire in my lungs.

Seeking attention for my efforts, upon my return home, I dramatically collapsed on the living room floor as if I'd run an ultra-marathon. Starting over was awful. There's no other way to put it.

But I was determined and I summoned up my internal over achiever to kick my own butt. I decided that getting outside and running would be a great way for me to see the French countryside. I wish I could say that I took Océane with me in the expensive jogging stroller that I bought online, but it turns out that jogging with one of those big strollers is a lot harder than those uber fit running-moms make it look. I made a new routine where I would go out running early in the morning before Kevin went to work, or sometimes he'd come home for lunch and hang out with Océane while I went for a quick training run. I set myself a goal and signed up for the Lindt Chocolate Factory Half Marathon. The factory was only about thirty minutes from our house and what more motivation did I need than a larger-than-life box of chocolates at the finish line to get me through the race.

It was about three months from my dramatic scene in the shoe closet, to lacing up for the half marathon, wearing significantly smaller underwear. The race was heavily male dominated as most races were in France, and I didn't care that I wasn't the fastest in the crowd. We all got the chocolate, so it didn't matter.

It started raining as I was driving out to the race with two girlfriends that were also running that day. Not ideal weather, but it beat snow. When we arrived we made a quick stop at the outdoor bathrooms and then planned to head to the starting line. Mid-pee, I hear a startling bang.

"Laurie, was that just the start gun?" I yelled loudly to my friend in the toilet next door.

"I think so," I heard her yell back, giggling as she always was.

"It's not funny. We're late. Let's go!" I said as I quickly tried to get out of the port-a-potty as fast as I could.

Unfortunately, the toilets were no way near the start line. We were sprinting in the rain for nearly an entire kilometre before we even reached the beginning of the race. Not exactly the start we had in mind.

After a round of running high fives we each continued at our own pace, planning to meet at the end and devour some chocolate.

I was really happy with my pace, and it looked like all my hard training was paying off. The freshness of the rain made me decide to leave my waist belt with my water back at the car because it wasn't that hot out and I was used to running without, so it wouldn't be a big deal. I knew there would be a few water stations along the way so I'd try and grab some water while I ran without breaking stride. I was a creature of habit and knew that once my legs slowed down or stopped they wouldn't want to start up again.

As I approached what I expected to be the water stand, I did a double take, then stopped dead in my tracks.

Prunes?

The table where I was expecting to get water was instead covered in snacks-to-go for the runners. There were loose raisins piled into a mountain on the table for people to grab a handful of. *Hello, germs! No thanks!* Beside the raisins were piles of prunes. This was almost laughable. Unless I wanted to poo my pants while I was running, I'd take a pass on the prunes. The last option was sugar cubes. The kind you plop into your tea if you're British. Yet, here they were acting as fuel to keep me going for another eighteen kilometres.

Without fully thinking it through, I grabbed a sugar cube, threw it down the hatch, and carried on running. Within three seconds of putting it into my mouth, it disintegrated and left me with a massive mouthful of sugar that I hadn't experienced since I was a kid hopped up on fun-dip. My knee-jerk reaction was to get it out fast. I spit, or more correctly, sprayed the sugar out of my mouth like a whale blowing water out of its blowhole. I was a sugary, sticky mess: not to mention, still thirsty.

Thankfully, it was raining enough that my hands actually got sufficiently wet enough to wash away the stickiness. I was also so wet that my phone, playing my 'keep running' music, stopped working.

As I rounded the corner at kilometre number fifteen, I stopped again, but this time I didn't care about breaking my stride. I knew they would come, and I intended on just sending a wave and carrying on. But when I saw Kevin standing there, holding Océane, who was now eight months old, up on his shoulders, telling her to yell, *"Allez, Maman.* Go, Mom!" I nearly burst into tears, and I'm not a crier. It must have been all the sugar playing with my emotions. I stopped running and wrapped them both up in a giant hug, then quickly remembered that if I stopped for too long, my legs wouldn't want to start again; so I carried on, turning back to yell to Kevin with a smile, "Her clothes don't match!" because they didn't.

Post-race you could find me chocolate-faced and flying high on running endorphins. I recounted the prune incident to Kevin on the ride home because I still couldn't believe that the people in charge actually planned that. Of all the things they could offer: gels packs, sliced oranges, water, electrolyte chews. Nope, none of those things sound like a good idea. Let's give the runners prunes instead… and throw in some straight up sugar cubes for good measure. At least we'd all be regular; but next time I'd be bringing what I need in my water belt.

What's a Nounou?

There were a lot of great things that we loved about living in France, and Europe for that matter. Our daily life felt like it slowed down... almost to the point where it was like we went back in time. Nobody stressed about things too much where we lived, and kids on our street still played outside until their parents called them in for dinner, around eight p.m. No one seemed to be in a hurry for anything.

We also loved having Europe as a home base for travel. We had easy access to so many countries at a fraction of the price that it cost to travel within North America. We were making the most of it, and Océane was a great little traveller.

The worst part about our new life was being so far from our families. Especially now that we had a baby. We had already done two trips back to Canada before Océane even turned one, but I couldn't help like feeling that she was missing out on time with her extended family. If we were back home she would have had tons of cousins her age to play with, and where we lived she was the only baby her age. I took her to playgroup once a week, but she was nearly a year now and she was starting to get 'busy'. I couldn't help but feel that she needed a little baby posse.

My internal crazies were coming out a bit and I had some new-mom paranoia. I didn't want to screw up my first child. I started over analysing the fact that she only spent time with me, and Kevin when he came home from work. Of course she needed to be with her mom and I knew that, but it had been almost a year and with no family around. If we were at home, she would have been passed around the kitchen from aunt to cousin to grandparent, to uncle and back through the list, but with a whole new set of faces. In our quiet little country life, she really only knew Kevin and I.

I just wished that *if* I should ever need to get away during the day, even for an hour, there would be someone I could trust leaving her with, like you would with family.

"Why don't you check your neighbourhood for a *nounou?*" one of the girls at playgroup suggested.

"What's a *nounou?*" I asked, trying to place the word.

"I guess it's what the French call a nanny," she offered.

I didn't need a nanny. I had no job. I wasn't about to get a nanny when I was home all day. And how weird would it be when Océane went for a nap, and I wanted to lazily hang out on the couch eating macarons and this 'nounou' would have to hang out with me. *No thanks.*

Over dinner I filled Kevin in on what the girls at playgroup had said, and he said that some ladies in his office also asked if we had a *nounou*. Apparently, after three months most French kids were in *creche*, which is daycare, or they had a *nounou*. So our child was clearly an anomaly having stayed home with me for ten months.

I dismissed the idea until it came up again about a month later.

"If you're still interested I've got more info on the *nounou* scene," Kevin mentioned as Océane covered her face in yogurt at the dinner table. "Apparently they don't come to your house, but you drop your baby off at their house, and they watch a few kids at once. The ladies at work said they watch three or four kids, so it's more like a child care provider than a nanny that comes to the house."

"Well, that sounds a bit more promising. I like the idea of her playing with other kids. But I don't know about leaving her yet," I told him. "If we did it, I'd only want her to go for a couple hours per week."

"And then you could go back to French classes," francophone Kevin cheerily piped in. He always gets excited at the idea of me brushing up my French.

"I agree, my French could definitely use some polishing. Look into it and let me know what you find," I said as I wiped the yogurt out of Océane's ears. "No weirdos though. I'll be checking these people out!" I yelled from the kitchen.

A couple days later Kevin came home with a list from the *Mairie*. City hall gives you a list of the names and numbers of the registered *nounous* in your neighbourhood, then you can contact them and see if they have space. Kevin got right to it and had an appointment for us that night to visit a lady that lived a few blocks away.

I sussed out the house and yard when we arrived, and my first impression was okay. We went in, and the lady seemed nice enough. We sat down and had a cup of tea in a room surrounded by transformers and monster trucks. The nounou watched two boys that were two years old, 'full of energy' she described them to us. I was a teacher. I knew what that meant. 'Full of energy' was a nice way of saying that they were wild. But they weren't there, so I couldn't judge for myself. As nice as this lady was, what was little Océane going to do there with two 'spirited' little boys that were double her age? It wouldn't have been the end of the world, and if we really needed a *nounou*, it could have worked. But this was a luxury, not a necessity, and I wasn't overly excited about the fit.

"You hated it in there," Kevin said as soon as we were in the secured silence of our car.

"No, I didn't *hate* it." I tried to search for something positive to say but the pause had become too long.

"We can keep looking." He gave me a sympathetic smile.

Two nights later we had a meeting with another *nounou* that lived just up the road from us. As we walked up the driveway, I didn't know it yet, but this house was about to become very familiar territory for me.

We rang the door bell, and from behind the door came this tiny woman, dressed amazingly, with a huge smile. She shot out her arms to the sides to welcome us like she had recognised us from somewhere.

"Ahhh! Les Canadiennes! Tu habites en face de ma mere!" The Canadians! You live across from my mom, she declared.

And then I recognised not her, but the vehicle out front. It was often parked across the street, and always gave a friendly little honk as it left. It was indeed a small town, or village, I guess.

Across the street from us lived a sweet elderly lady that Océane would later come to know as *Mammie,* what French kids call their Grandmas. At this point I referred to her as *Madame* because I could never remember her last name and I had to call her something.

"Bonjour, Madame!" I would call across the street as we both went out to check our mail.

That was about the extent of our solo conversations but Kevin had spoken to her a few times and said that Madame's son and his family lived next door to us, on the left. Turns out this family had a monopoly on the street.

"Entré, entré!" Come in, come in, *nounou* welcomed us at the front door, kissing us both twice on the cheeks.

"Vous êtes Corinne, oui?" Kevin confirmed that her name was Corinne. He was right, but she insisted that we call her Coco, like everyone else did. *Coco Chanel*, I thought in my head, trying to relate it to something I wouldn't forget. She was definitely the first Coco I'd ever met, but not the last. I lived in France now, after all.

We walked into the kitchen, and Kevin complimented her on their house. Rightly so, as it was really nice, and quite different from your typical French home. Which made sense because she then told us that her husband built it himself.

"Cheri," she affectionately called for him in a sing-song voice.

Out came Antoine, her husband, greeting us with *les bisous*. Followed by their three daughters, each politely introducing themselves and also giving us *les bises*. Five of them, with two kisses each, times two of us, makes for twenty rapid-fire kisses exchanged in true French fashion as we entered their home.

Coco showed us around the house, and the yard with a pool, that had a locked fence for safety, a playhouse, slide, swing set, trampoline, and a playroom inside full of toys. The house itself was immaculately kept. There wasn't a mess in sight. She explained that she watched two other little girls, one three months older than Océane, and one that was two months younger. She scooped our baby up in her arms, tickling her and covering her in kisses like she'd known her forever. Océane was laughing and sat happily on her hip as we were shown the house and got to know our neighbours a bit better.

This place was perfect. I was sold at the flurry of kisses when we walked in.

"You liked that one!" Kevin said with a smile bordering laughter, just because he knew me so well.

We called Coco back the next day, even though she told us to let her know by the following week. We told her we definitely wanted the spot. We started out by me bringing Océane over for a visit one morning, so she could get to know the other little girls while I had coffee with Coco. There was no English spoken in the house, so this was just as good as any French lesson for me. Coffee with Coco meant an hour of intensive one-on-one French. Having been home playing the new-mom role, I hadn't regularly spoken much French since my power dates in Paris with my French teacher so the hour of French, without any wine involved, was challenging. The two little girls that Coco watched welcomed their new playmate and the three of them squealed in delight the whole time. We'd made a good decision.

Two days later we went back, and after some kisses on the cheeks and French chat, we did a trial run where I left Océane there for an hour, went out and got some groceries by myself for the first time in almost a year and came back.

"Pas de problème," she said with a smile as I came back an hour later, or maybe a bit sooner because of new-mom nerves.

That settled it then. Océane had been integrated without so much as a hiccup, and I was a French student for three mornings a week, *encore.*

Paris, My Old Friend

It's my 40th Birthday! We're going to have a big party and you have to come! You can stay with me. It'll be a ton of fun. Please say yes!?!
Love Sharon

I walked away from my laptop, heading in Kevin's direction, thinking. I really missed my yoga friends in Paris, but I didn't know if I was ready to leave Océane overnight just yet.

Kevin was in the kitchen, staring inside the refrigerator, deciding what he wanted to eat. Whenever I see him doing this, I always hear my Dad's voice in my head telling me to close the fridge. I refrained from nagging because as long as he wasn't melting the ice cream, I didn't really care.

"I just got an email from Sharon."

"Oh ya? What's new with her?" He grabbed a brick of cheese.

"It's her fortieth and she wants me to go to Paris for her party."

"You should go," he encouraged me, far more easily than I probably would have done had the tables been turned and I was being left home and missing out on a trip to Paris.

"But I can't leave Océane. And, you of course, but you know… she's so little." I was waffling.

"It'll be good for you. I'll be here with Océane. She'll be fine. Go email Sharon." He nodded his head back towards my computer, smiling.

"Are you sure?" I asked, grabbing a piece of cheese he'd cut for himself and quickly sliding it into my mouth.

"Go." He laughed.

Just like that I decided I'd go, but I really was nervous about leaving my baby over night for the first time. With a little self-talk, I calmed myself down because I knew that she'd be okay with Kevin. He was a good dad, or *Papa* as Océane just started calling him. I would just go for one night to minimise my guilt.

Sharon was thrilled, and promised it would be a great time.

The flight to Paris was only an hour, but it felt so weird to be boarding a plane alone. It seemed like forever since I'd done that. No diaper bag, no changes of clothes. I only *just* became okay with leaving Océane for a few hours a week to go down the street to my French classes, and now I was on a plane, alone. It was a creepy sort of freedom that I wasn't yet sure what to do with.

I took a deep breath, told myself to relax and enjoy it. I only had about thirty-six hours.

The plan was that I'd make my way to Sharon's, drop off my stuff, and spend the day doing Paris-things. I was hoping to go to my favourite restaurant in the Marais for lunch and maybe do a bit of shopping. Then I had to go to the Champ de Mars and pick up my race package for *La Feminine* race the next morning. I'd be running the annual six kilometre ladies race through Paris that I ran when we lived there. It's the same time each year, so when I realised it was on the weekend of Sharon's birthday, it was all the more reason to go.

Sharon's apartment was perfectly located in the third arrondissement, which was great for me because that's the area of Paris I knew best. After months of walking the neighbourhood streets near the yoga studio, the Marais was practically like my own neighbourhood. So much so that after dropping off my bags, I knew exactly what I wanted to do with my day.

I had a quick lunch and then was going to visit an old friend. As I opened up the door to his store, a smile spread across his face. "You're back!" he said in French, stopping what he was doing to come over and greet me with *la bises.*

I went to my favourite purse shop that I had stumbled on when we first moved to Paris. Without knowing it, I was shopping in the wholesale district, meaning that these shops were only for people who stocked and supplied to stores. I couldn't get over the amazing prices of these handbags. They were far cheaper than anywhere else, and they were really nice.

Without a moment's hesitation, I grabbed one in every colour, and style, for everyone I knew and had created a mountain of purses, piled high beside the cash register.

Then the formalities began, and he asked me what shop I supplied for, because with the amount I was buying, I could have filled an entire store. I was confused at first because my French wasn't great at the time, and with a lot of charades we determined that I indeed, did *not* work for a supplier. I just loved handbags. When the man saw the joy on my face crumble, he must have taken pity on me, because he let me buy the bags anyway.

I quickly learned that no other stores in this wholesale neighbourhood will let you shop there. Many have signs in the window, which I couldn't read at the time, but my friend the purse peddler was always happy to have me back. Every time I went back to Canada, I'd bring half a suitcase full of handbags as gifts for my mom, sister-in-laws and friends.

As I once again piled purses high on his counter, he asked me how my baby was and complimented me on how much my French had improved.

"A bientôt!" he said with a smile as he held the door open for me so I could get out of the shop without dropping my bags full of bags.

I clearly couldn't go pick up my race package carrying all these purses, so I had to make a pit stop back at Sharon's to dump them in my suitcase.

"I was wondering why you brought such a giant suitcase for just one night. You planned ahead," she said as she opened the door to the apartment, letting me in.

I only had to walk a couple blocks, but the bags were so heavy that my hands were shaking and stuck in the curved position of carrying the bags, even once I had already put them down.

"Ya, I brought the big suitcase for the bags and I also have four outfit options for tonight in there," motioning toward my suitcase. "Each with their own pair of shoes. I couldn't decide what to wear so I just basically brought my closet. You can help me choose later."

With a quick turn around time, I was back out the door and on the Metro heading for Champ des Mars. As I came up the stairs from underground and rounded the corner, I couldn't help but smile. That view of the Eiffel Tower just didn't get old.

I collected my race pack, checked out the free shirt inside, perused a few of the booths set up in the race village and then made my way back to Sharon's.

"Okay, what do we have to get done for tonight?" I asked, ready to put myself to work.

"Not much, we'll make a couple snacks, and apparently you have a fashion show waiting for me in your suitcase," she said with a smile.

"Right. But I almost forgot. I brought something to make for the party. It's my Canadian specialty."

Sharon, being from the States, was curious. When you've lived outside your own country for so long, it's always nice to have something from home. And since Canada and the US were practically sisters, I had a feeling that at one point in her life, she might have been familiar with my special treat.

I re-emerged from the bedroom holding a bottle of vodka in one hand and two boxes of Canadian imported jello in the other.

"Jello shooters!" She laughed. "You're hilarious. Those will be a big hit."

"And I even brought some veggie-friendly gelatine too." I came prepared.

With the jello shooters setting, the snacks made, and the fashion show under way, Sharon's daughter wished us a good night as she got picked up by a friend's mom for a sleepover. She was kind enough to give me permission to sleep in her bed for the night, as long as I looked after her guinea pig. I didn't let her know how much I'm not an animal person, but agreed that the little creature would be in good hands. Although not mine, because I didn't plan on touching it.

The first guests to arrive were the yoga girls, where I was wrapped in hugs, and squeals of delighted surprise echoed the room since neither Sharon or I had told them I was in town. It was Sharon's big day, but she let me share the spotlight a bit when she decided we should surprise the other girls.

As the night went on, Sharon's playlist got a little louder, the lighting got a little darker and her living room turned into a happening dance floor, looking out at beautiful Parisian balconies of the neighbouring apartments. There was an interesting group of people mixing and mingling, from the boisterous chef, to the Disney producer; all equally happy to sample my Canadian speciality and all unanimously commenting on how heavy handed I was when adding the vodka to the recipe.

The next morning my alarm beeped loudly, and I turned it off as quickly as my slow-moving body could manage. Needing a little fresh air, I cracked open the window and lay back down.

'Good luck on the run,' Sharon texted me from the other room. My alarm clock had clearly woken her too.

"I'm not going," I shouted back.

"Seriously?" There was now a pinch of humour in her voice. "Is it that bad?"

"Maybe I'll just lie still for a few minutes and see if I feel any better."

A few minutes turned into about half an hour and guilt was starting to get the better of me.

"I can hear them," Sharon called back. We were two lazy zombies, calling down the hall to each other.

"I know, me too. I have to close the window, so I stop feeling bad about not being out there." With thirty-thousand women warming up for a race at the bottom of the Eiffel Tower, the sound and excitement was easily carried into the apartment.

I could barely make it out of bed to close the window; I was clearly in no shape to run a race. And with that I went back to sleep and pretended the race never happened.

Let Me Buy You That Bumper

A few months had passed and Océane was loving being at nounou's. Coco had become like part of our family, and we became part of theirs. We were getting to know our neighbours to our left and '*Mammie*' across the street much better too. My French was also improving greatly, not just because of my classes but talking so much with Coco gave me the confidence to just say whatever I thought was right. Half the time it probably wasn't, but she was too nice to tell me otherwise, and we worked it out and figured out a way to communicate.

My friend Katrina (the one who swept through my house with the broom after that first playgroup when I was pregnant) was heading home to Australia for a visit, which meant that she had to hit up the Lindt factory to load up her suitcase with chocolatey gifts to bring back.

I arrived at French class that morning only to find out it was cancelled, and I had already dropped Océane off at Coco's. With a few free hours on my hands I knew exactly what I wanted to do.

I reached for my phone. "Have you left yet?" I asked Katrina, hoping she hadn't.

"No. I'm running late. I'll be heading out in about fifteen minutes."

We made a plan for her to meet at my place since it was on the way, then we only had to take one car. Look at us; I went from sitting in my air-conditioned car going nowhere with the motor running, to being an eco-warrior, car sharing to the Lindt factory. Katrina arrived and I grabbed my purse, eager to get on the road.

"Want me to drive?" I asked.

"Ya, sure. Thanks, mate."

I grabbed my keys, hopped in my car that was in the exact spot in our driveway that I always parked and started the engine. The problem with that exact spot where I always park was that there was usually nothing behind me. I put the car in reverse, gave a haphazard glance over my shoulder and dropped my heavy foot on the gas.

BOOM

"What was that?" I questioned Katrina who was beside me in the passenger seat.

"I think it was my car," she said flatly, but too scared to turn around and look.

I got out to assess the damage.

There's a few things to point out in this situation. Katrina had a really nice car. And ours wasn't too bad either. Really nice cars tend to be more expensive to fix. That was not good news.

Another thing to note. Katrina's husband, Kurt, worked with Kevin. They were actually office neighbours, so they talked often. News was going to travel fast.

We stared at each other blankly, wondering how we were going to play this one.

"Who should we call first?" she asked.

"I should go first; it was my fault." I was not looking forward to this conversation. We sat in my car and Katrina gave me a 'good luck' face as we both heard the phone ringing through the quietness of the car.

"Oui, allo." Kevin picked up the phone like a true French person.

"Hey, it's me," I said sheepishly on the other end of the line.

"What happened?" Man, he knew me well!

"It's not good." I cringed.

I could hear him let out a big sigh but he didn't say anything, so I just blurted out, "I drove our car into Kurt and Katrina's."

"What?"

"Did you not hear me or…"

"I heard you, Lis." He was slightly exasperated, but not as bad as I thought. "How did you manage to do that? We have reverse sensors on our car."

It was true. The car beeped when you got too close to something, but that only works if you're going slow enough to notice before it's too late, which I was not. Without even giving me a chance to answer he figured that out on his own.

"How fast were you pulling out of the driveway?" Quickly followed by, "Was Océane with you?"

"No, she was at Coco's and our car's not *that* bad." I avoided the question about my speed and I also avoided saying anything about Kurt and Katrina's car. But he was onto me.

"What about Kurt's car?"

"His bumper is lying on our driveway."

"Lisa!"

Just as he knew me all too well, I also knew how embarrassed he was going to be heading into his colleague's office and telling him that his car just got wrecked, by his wife. He was guilty by association, and I did feel bad.

We got off the phone, and I knew he wasn't mad, but more frustrated at the pending mountain of French paper work this was going to cause.

"Your turn?" I asked Katrina.

I hung up the phone, and she called her husband and didn't get past, "I'm here with Lisa, and..."

"Oh no, what happened? Kev just walked in and he's making a face." I could hear Kurt through the phone, and by the chuckle in his voice I knew neither of us were in too deep of hot water. But I could just picture them: Kurt at his desk taking it all in, while Kev leaned against the door frame, shaking his head in a combination of disbelief and mild embarrassment.

In the following weeks the boys had several lunch dates at the office, spilling themselves over the piles of insurance paper hoops that needed to be jumped through to file a claim. If there was one thing the French loved, it was testing people's sanity limits with unimaginable amounts of paper work. Since Kevin has handled all of our bureaucracy since moving, I always tell him that nothing ever gets done without him needing a copy of our family tree, a blood sample and a photocopy of his right testicle. He thinks it's a bit graphic (and only slightly exaggerated), but try and get anything done at a government level in this country and tell me I'm wrong.

Tripping Over My French

Dealing with the car getting fixed meant that it was a good time to make sure all of my paper work was up to date since we had every legal document we owned spread across our kitchen table. I needed to renew my *Carte de sejour* which meant we'd be staying in France longer, but I hated even thinking about the line I was going to have to stand in at the *prefecture* office.

I had it made when I was pregnant. In Paris it didn't matter if I was trying on a T-shirt at H&M or joining the back of the two-hour line to go up the Eiffel Tower; people saw I was pregnant and I would get whisked to the front. Always. Without exception.

At first the polite Canadian in me was too timid to exercise this privilege. I'd wait patiently in line like everyone else, and when I'd get to the front and someone would see me, I would almost get scolded for waiting in line. This happened to me all the time in Paris. Later in my pregnancy, when we were getting a lot of visitors, and I was getting bigger and bigger, I decided to take the French up on this 'no line' business and see how it worked for me.

It was fabulous. I usually didn't even need to speak, I'd just approach the front of the line, belly first, and the person working would part the seas of tourists for my guests and I to enter. I'm talking the Louvre, Eiffel Tower, Notre Dame, Versailles, Euro Disney, airport check-in and security. I even had luck on a trip to the Vatican and that's a serious line up! Europe in the summer has lines that make you question why you came in the first place. Being pregnant in Paris, it was like having an all-access VIP pass to the city.

Tourist attractions are great, but I usually just went to those places when we had visitors. The real golden ticket for me was the grocery store when we left Paris. As soon as we settled into our village outside Pau, we quickly took to living the quiet French country life. But we needed a car to get around, unlike Paris. This meant no more lugging my groceries home in a cart. I could drive to the grocery store and fill my trunk with food. It made me feel at home just to see a parking lot again. There's no space for that kind of luxury in Paris. Although I still shopped at local markets, butchers and bakeries, the North American in me loved going to the big box grocery store to really stock up the house as if we were waiting for a natural disaster.

The grocery store I always went to had a special line for pregnant women. There's a sign above the checkout indicating whether that particular checkout was for pregnant women or people with health issues that needed extra care. If there's no one there, others are welcome to use it, however, first priority was given to those it was intended for.

Since I got accustomed to the Parisian way, I was no longer shy when it came to claiming my line-cutting privileges when I was pregnant. It almost became a habit for me. That just became the line I used, even after Océane was born and if someone who was pregnant or needed the line showed up, I'd naturally let them in front of me, just how so many people did for me.

This brings me to the first of three very embarrassing incidents that had taken place since we left Paris, the line-cutting, city of lights.

Language Barrier Number One

Even though my French had improved, I still found myself struggling every now and then when I was put on the spot and couldn't find the right word. I was at the grocery store stocking up and Océane wasn't wanting to go for a 'ride' in the cart, which was odd for her. I chalked it up to teething, as I did anytime anything went wrong, and strapped her into the baby carrier that I had in the cart. She was happy and I could still go in and get some groceries. A bit too comfy in the carrier and she was out like a light, having a morning nap, while I went about my shopping. It was fine with me as I was enjoying the snuggle, until it came time to unload the cart.

When I got to the bottom of the cart, I could barely reach the items I needed to put on the checkout belt. I was cradling Océane's head with one hand, so it wouldn't wobble around, and unloading the cart with the other.

Of course the lady at the cash would not start checking through my groceries until we did the mandatory polite exchange and then I'd give her the green light to start. I was running out of space and I couldn't catch the lady's eye to say, '*Bonjour*'. One-handedly, I continued my unloading while cranking my neck around, finally catching her eye and telling her, "*Bonjour, allez-y'"* Let's get things moving.

I finally reached the bottom of the cart, sweating now, and of course having to practise my second language is just what I'm put for. The cashier said something along the lines of, 'Good work emptying all that with your hands so full.'

I thanked her and my reply was not the natural banter I'd have in English. Instead my mind quickly searched for the proper French grammar, and I tried for something along the lines of, *"Yes, thanks! It's difficult only using one hand."* She awkwardly smiled at me and continued scanning my groceries, saying nothing further until she gave me my total.

Later that night I was reading Océane a story that happened to be in French. Those ones are usually reserved for Kevin, but this one was simple enough, so we sat on the couch looking through this picture book about body parts. As we flipped the pages we arrived at one showing arms and legs, and I realised my error.

"Uuuggghhh," I groaned, throwing back my head and covering my face with my hands.

Kevin popped out from around the corner to see what I was moaning about.

"I told the woman working at the grocery store that I only have one leg! *And* I was in the special needs checkout!"

Kevin never had to worry about moments like this, but tried to be sympathetic and turn down the smile creeping up on his lips.

I told the girls the next morning and there was a unanimous feeling of empathy, followed by a list of 'I once said' scenarios to make me feel better. The life of a foreigner didn't seem to be getting any easier.

Language Barrier Number Two

Just when I was getting over the humiliation of the grocery store incident I was hit with another one.

Coco was used to me blundering the French language by now, and she was perfectly fine with it, which was one of the reasons I loved her. That and the fact that she always looked good enough to go to a party, even though she worked from home. If I had an appointment and would need to bring Océane there first thing in the morning, she would be dressed, makeup on and hair done, walking around her house in four-inch heels, even though she wasn't even going to be leaving the house. This was typically French. No matter how hard you try, you will never see a French person out in public in jogging pants. Coco, however, had seen me in jogging pants on more than one occasion. *Yoga pants actually, so that's much better, right?*

I had French class on Tuesday morning, but Océane woke up not feeling well. She had a really high temperature, so I texted Coco and told her that I'd be staying home, and I didn't need to bring Océane over that morning.

The next day Coco texted me to see how she was feeling. Océane was much better, and I tried to let her know via text, but it turns out *this* is how our conversation went.

Coco: *Comment est Océane aujourd'hui?* How is Océane?

Me: *Pas 100% mais elle est meurt hier soir.* Not 100% but she died last night.

Coco: *Quoi??* What?

Then my phone rang instantly.

Coco had a confused panic in her voice that I hadn't heard before. When she heard me sounding chipper and happy, she questioned what I was trying to tell her in my text message. I explained again that she wasn't perfect, but she was better than last night. Breathing a huge sigh of relief, Coco explained that although they sound similar, '*meilleur*' which I meant to text, meant better. But '*meurt*', what I actually texted, meant dead. I blame auto-correct, but now know that one misspelled word can really change the context of a conversation.

Language Barrier Number Three

I swear this all happened within a couple of weeks, which was probably a sign that I should ramp up my French classes. But I saved the best example for last, so brace yourself.

We were having plumbing issues in our house, so Kevin called someone to come by while he was at work and have a look. He called and asked that I made sure to be home that afternoon because a plumber was coming by to see what was wrong. Océane always napped in the afternoon so it wasn't going to be a problem.

When the man arrived, I greeted him and explained the issues as best I could, but he had already talked to Kevin on the phone, so he was ready to go about his business.

I told him to make himself at home and let me know if he needed anything. I carried on my phone call with my mom, and he went around the house, checking toilets and sinks, then went puttering in the yard. After a while of him in and out of the house, he said he needed to talk to me. I told my mom I'd call her back, and the plumber said something to me in French that I didn't understand at all. He repeated himself, but all I could get the gist of was him telling me not to put something in the toilet. *Well, that's obvious. I only put toilet 'things' in the toilet.*

The part I didn't understand was what it was that shouldn't go in there, and why. He motioned for me to follow him outside. It seemed weird but I did anyway.

He started looking around the yard, then grabbed a stick from the side bushes and told me to follow him. Our property was fairly large, and we made our way to the back corner, just myself, Mr Plumber, and the stick. What he was planning on doing with the stick, I had no idea.

After a few charades and some pointing, I figured out that our house was on a septic tank. I had no idea before then and that was definitely not something that was in my French vocabulary. I'd never needed to use the word in English, never mind French. And besides, we were only one kilometre outside town. I'd only ever heard of people living really far out in the country having those. But we were in rural-ish France and maybe the plumbing was different here.

What he did next will forever be etched in my mind. You can't erase things like that.

With stick in hand, he leaned down to open a cement cover in the ground.

No? He wasn't going to…

He put his stick into the septic tank, and I waited in horror to find out what in the world he was up to. My face was distorted and my nose let my brain know what was in that hole.

Why is he in there?

With a few twirls and jerks of the stick, like he was trying to hook a fish, he seemed satisfied with himself and lifted his stick out of the tank to show me what he had caught.

My face, that was once scrunched up from the awful smell had now fallen, jaw open and skin stark white in disbelief. He had caught a tampon. Not just any, out of the box, tampon. He had caught a used tampon, that had been sitting in a septic tank for who knows how long? I thought I might vomit.

"Vous comprendrez maintenant?" He asked if I now understood.

Paralysed with mental trauma as if I'd just walked in on my parents having sex, I wanted to turn and run, but I just stood there, disgusted, horrified, and unable to speak. I nodded my head in agreement that I understood and that I would no longer put tampons down the toilet. Easier said than done when I'd been doing it since I was in early adolescence. I can't say I didn't have any slip-ups after his visit. But you can be sure that as soon as I realised what I'd done (usually mid-flush) I prayed with all my might that that sucker would make it down without causing any trouble. The last thing I wanted was to go on another fishing trip with the plumber.

The moral I took away from these language barriers was 'learn the damn language'! It would have saved me a lot of embarrassing moments and confusion if my French was better. And had the words 'septic' and 'tank' been in my vocabulary, I'd be a lot better off today, because you can't un-see something like that.

Ready, Set, Eat!

I always find it to be a strange and slightly awkward situation when you arrive to a gathering of expats that live in France.

We all know that it's mandatory to greet people with *les bisous* in a French environment, but what happens if you're in France, but none of the people you're meeting are French? Do you still do *la bise*? I was from Canada, the other person might be from England, and we're double-kissing like French people.

This is what happened when we were invited to a dinner party at Kurt and Katrina's. Our regular expat crowd was all present, but without their kids. Normally we'd get together as families, but it was a special occasion and we were doing something a little different, so everyone got a babysitter. It was Kurt's birthday, and Katrina had hired a French chef to come to their house and cook us dinner. It was all very swanky, and so quiet without the culmination of about fifteen kids between us that were usually running around.

Aurelie called up as usual, checking to see what time she should pick us up. She always drove because she lived further out of town and a taxi ride out to her place was the equivalent of a week's groceries, *if* you could persuade one to go out there.

"Is eight good for me to pick you guys up tonight?" she asked.

"Actually... I'm going to drive tonight, so we'll just see you there. Thanks though."

"What?" I think that was directed at me, but it's always hard to tell when you're talking to a mom with a toddler in the background.

"Yup, I'll just see you there. Thanks for the offer!" and I got off the phone quicker than I normally would.

Kevin and I arrived at Kurt and Katrina's to a mixture of handshakes, waves from across the room, hugs and, of course, *la bise.* Once you're here for long enough, the double kiss starts to feel normal and, yes, you just do it to people, French or not.

"Happy Birthday, Kurt!" Kevin said, shaking his hand at the door. "Hope you're enjoying your gift, the new bumper," he said with a smile.

"We've got tons of Champagne on ice in the kitchen. Come on in!" Katrina said, leading us towards the bubbles.

"Actually, I brought my own. I'll just go ahead and open it; don't worry about me," I told her. But she was quick and knew something was up. She took the bottle from my hand and had a look at the label.

"D'Artingy?!" she said in an octave higher than she was speaking before. She knew that was the non-alcoholic Champagne that I discovered at the end of my first pregnancy. Looking at me strangely for a moment and then plastering a giant smile across her face, she pulled me in for a hug. "You've caught the 'tummy bug'!" she whispered in my ear, delighted!

Katrina was already three months pregnant, and so was Aurelie. I was about thirty seconds pregnant at the time, but with this group, and me saying no to Champagne, there was no point in trying to hide it.

I started suggesting to Kev when Océane was nine months old that maybe we should have another baby. He looked at me like I was crazy, motioned to our little peanut in her car seat and told me we already had a baby. *Fair enough, she was barely moving yet.* I dropped a couple more hints over the following months, and by the time Océane was blowing out her first birthday candle, her sibling was on the way.

With Aurelie standing close by, it didn't take long for her to catch wind of the news, rushing over with a huge smile. "I knew there was a reason you were driving!"

Word travelled fast through the crowded house and before I knew it, Mary had filled my glass with D'Artingy and we were toasting to Baby Webb number two.

"Okay, okay, that's enough of me stealing the show! It's Kurt's birthday, not my baby shower; what's this chef cooking up for us? I'm eating for two now, so bring it on!"

I took a look at the menu on one of the place settings.

Verrine de soupe aux petits pois
Toast de ladro maison de cochon noir de Bigorre
Tataki beef, quince cheese and foie gras kebab
Scallops
Peas and bacon with magret de canard
Braised rabbit with rosemary, olives and tomatoes
Wrinkly new potatoes and young carrots
Birthday cake!

This is what I love about being a community of mixed cultures. The fact that the menu was half in French and half in English, was not weird, but heartwarming. Talk about knowing your crowd. Well played, chef!

I took a seat as we were called to the table, so the chef could begin serving. I'd say it was probably around eight thirty, or twenty hours thirty if you were being French. This was a standard time to begin dinner in France. You won't find a restaurant in town that is open before seven p.m. A few let you in at seven thirty, but you'll be hanging out alone until eight. If you think this is late, you should have seen our shock when we first crossed the border to Spain. I was ready for bed by the time the restaurants began showing any signs of accepting guests. No wonder they need an afternoon siesta!

The courses started being served and my non-alcoholic Champagne wasn't nearly as exciting as some of the wines accompanying the food, but missing out on amazing French wine wasn't new to me. So far, I'd been pregnant for more time in France than not, so it was a good thing I'd become acquainted with D'Artingy. It beats sitting down at an amazing dinner with a glass of water; at least I felt like I was joining in.

But the problem with being the one, or in this case, one of the three, not drinking, is that you miss out on that little wine buzz that makes you want to stay up all night having fun.

By the time the chef served the birthday cake it was one fifteen a.m. I know this because I checked the time on my phone. Normally, at a wine-infused dinner party, I'm chatting my neighbour's ear off, but tonight my bum had been soberly sat in the chair for nearly five hours. The food was amazing, the company was great, but I was sober as a judge and getting a sore bottom.

The night rounded down as the pregnant ladies led the way out the door, keys in hand, thanking Kurt, Katrina and the chef for such an amazing night. For their sake, I hope he stuck around to clean all the dishes.

This marathon dinner party should have prepared us a bit for the French way of eating. It's an art, an enjoyment, and a drawn-out process that can last, as I now know, for hours on end.

Coco and Antoine invited us over for lunch on Sunday, a few weeks later. What I love about this small-town life is that they were just leaving their mom's across the street, and saw Kevin and Océane playing in the yard, and shouted across the street, "Hey, why don't you guys stop by for lunch today."

They casually agreed that we'd stop by around noon, and it was settled; over two fences and a road, we now had plans for lunch, with the only instructions being for us to bring our swimsuits. Hopefully their pool didn't have the same strict dress code as the public pools.

We walked over a couple hours later, and as usual, were greeted by a flurry of kisses crossing all members of each family. It was a beautiful day, with summer stretching into fall. Warm autumns were something that this Canadian wasn't used to. Océane, who felt at home at Coco's by now, had toddled off to play with Coco's daughters, feeling very grown up, and we made our way to the backyard to greet a few other friends that they had invited over.

A combination of being able to uninhibitedly practise my French with Coco regularly, and hearing Kevin speaking to Océane in French at home, meant that my language skills were slowly coming along. It was full on immersion in our neighbourhood and this lunch was no exception. However, without any liquid courage, and not knowing these people, made me a bit more shy than I would be in an English setting. I always feel like I should introduce myself by saying, "Hi I'm Lisa. Sorry for my terrible French." But everyone was nice, and didn't seem to mind that I was probably butchering their language, so I relaxed and enjoyed myself.

Coco, seeing me regularly throughout the week, suspected something was up with me when I started looking like the walking dead when I'd dropped Océane off to go to my French class.

"Tu vas bien? Qu'est-ce quise passe?" Are you okay? What's going on? She'd drilled me one morning. And because my secret was already out, I told her that there was going to be one more French-Canadian in the neighbourhood soon. She was thrilled, wrapped me up in more kisses and said something in Spanish, as she sometimes does, from Antoine's influence over the years.

Knowing I wouldn't be joining in the festivities, she grabbed Kevin a beer and showed me her supply of Fanta, Orangina, Perrier, and Coke. Because people still drink Coke in France. I poured myself a Perrier and promptly started drooling as I caught a glance of what Antoine was carrying over to the grill. His Spanish-inspired, outdoor kitchen, was a project he'd just finished the year before. It was beautifully made of stone, and it was big enough to fit enough food to feed the neighbourhood, which seemed to be what they were doing. His stone oven belonged in a magazine, and so did the food that was about to be placed on top. There was tray after tray of shrimp, lamb, sausages, chicken, peppers, zucchinis and onions. Not to mention the table that had an array of salads and a pile of fresh baguettes. We had our work cut out for us.

Just like the French dinner party we were at a few weeks earlier, the eating lasted a long time, which was okay for me, because I like to eat. This wasn't a formal sit-down dinner with a chef, and with kids around, it meant that I wasn't in my seat the whole time. Antoine would grill, we would eat, they would all drink, music was playing, Coco was dancing and kids were in and out of the pool. We didn't have any 'real' family in France, but aside from the bloodline, this felt pretty close to family to me! We felt like we were at a BBQ at home, and couldn't be happier that we had stumbled across 'Madame' across the street and all her family.

By four the outdoor speakers were now housing some lovely karaoke for all the neighbours to enjoy, and Antoine had finally persuaded Kevin to have a try at his bow and arrow. They had a big yard, with a proper target practice at one end. Kevin, being bigger than your average French man, was a crowd pleaser, just as he was at the village fair.

Océane was inside napping, and if my nose didn't deceive me, someone had started up the grill again. I felt like I was going to burst, but I was correct and the outdoor stone oven was back in use. In true French fashion, we needed our post-meal cheese course. Two giant wheels of Camembert were left in their containers and placed on the grill. This being my second pregnancy in France, I knew by now which cheeses were pasteurised and which were not; this cheese was good to get in my belly. One slice of the knife over the top of the Camembert revealed the most delicious, gooey, cheesy heaven that you could imagine. With pieces of baguette in hand, we began dipping in to this cheesy dream, that I would soon come to create regularly for dinner guests of our own. Looks like I was becoming French after all.

With the kids on the swing sets and me lying like a garden gnome on the lawn, I couldn't fathom that there might be another course coming. The French love dessert and it had yet to appear, which was fine by me, because I couldn't even think of food at this point.

By eight p.m. we'd had dessert and by nine we were making our way back home, stuffed, from the longest lunch we'd ever experienced in our lives. Good thing we liked these people and they were good fun, or that could have been really painful.

"Did you have fun?" Kevin said to me with a smile, as we walked down the street towards our house.

"I did," I replied. "But next time, I might have to bring my PJs."

Recovering Germaphobe

It was another lazy weekend Chez Webb. The weather was still nice, and we were deciding how we should spend the rest of our day.

We'd already taken a trip to *Les Halles,* the market, which was becoming a bit of a weekend ritual. I loved strolling through the fruit and vegetable vendors, seeing what was fresh and what kind of deals I could get each week. We'd pick up all sorts of cheeses, which the ladies working behind the counter would have Océane sample as we went. They were always as delighted to see her, as she was them. Kevin would usually get some sort of meat from the butcher to grill later in the day, and we'd often have breakfast at the *creperie,* across from Kevin's favourite espresso stop.

This Saturday was much like any other, but we felt like getting outside since the weather was so nice. With warm crepes in our bellies, we were back home and decided that after Océane got up from her nap we would take her to the zoo for a few hours. To be clear, it wasn't a zoo as much as an outdoor park with a bit of wildlife. But she was one and a half years old, the bar to impress her was set pretty low.

"We should watch the video Coco made for us while we're waiting for Océane to get up," I suggested, remembering she put it in Océane's bag the day before.

"Sure, I'll go get it." Kevin put in the video, and I curled up into my regular spot on the couch.

Coco loved taking pictures of the kids she watched, and twice a year she made video DVDs out of the kids' pictures, put to music. Each of the kids got their own video/music montage. Being as sweet as she was, Coco asked me what songs I liked because she wanted to put some English music on Océane's video for me, but since she couldn't speak English, she had no idea what to choose. I told her not to worry about me, any music that she liked would be fine with me.

As the video begins, Océane's little face is staring back at us with a song that makes me want to cry, even though I've only heard a few words. I couldn't help but feel emotional as I watched the pictures of our daughter, how she'd grown so much in such a short amount of time.

"Is she purposely trying to make me cry?" My two-hundred-and-forty-pound, sensitive husband said and he quickly wiped the tears from the corners of his eyes.

The song she paired the pictures with was a French tear jerker about a father watching his daughter grow and about how much her loves her. Apparently it was a famous one, lost on me, but clearly pulled at Kevin's heart strings. As the next song played, I realised that she indeed did put an English song on there for my benefit. How very sweet of her.

'We're over. We're through. I don't love you any more,' the video sang out in a slow hate-ballad, while flashing pictures of Océane's little face.

Kevin and I looked at each other, eyes wide, trying not to laugh because she meant well, but had no idea what the words of the video were saying. It was probably the worst match that could ever be picked for a video of baby pictures.

"Are you going to tell her?" Kevin asked.

"Not a chance!" Even though she told me that she'd change the songs if I didn't like them, she worked so hard, and tried to be so thoughtful that I loved the video just the way it was. And I'm sure that I've done much worse with my French. At least it would make us smile whenever we watched it.

Shortly after our break-up video of Océane, she was up from her nap, and we made the half-hour drive to the animal park. By Canadian standards this would not even qualify as a zoo, but since living in France our standards have been lowered in some areas and raised in others. If we're going to a restaurant and were comparing wine, cheese, bread, or any type of food really, we've now gotten used to the way things are done in France and may very well have to change our expectations when in Canada. At the same time, things like cleanliness in public washrooms, having garbage and recycling readily available anywhere you go, I'd have to say that it took a bit of adjusting for me when we moved to France.

In my 'past life' when I worked in an elementary school, I was surrounded by germs. Kids would come into my office and sneeze all over my desk, including into my cup of tea. This was just a hazard of the job. It caused me to become a germaphobe without even realising it. I was washing my hands constantly. Not like a regular person, hitting the soap and water after going to the bathroom, but I'd wash my hands *before* going to the bathroom, to get the kid-germs off, then revisit the sink after going to the washroom. And I obviously *never* touched the door handle on the way out. That's what paper towel was for!

Most public bathrooms in Calgary, where we lived in Canada, were modern and set up for germ freaks like me, designing malls and airports so everything was automated and you didn't have to touch a thing. The soap dispensed on its own, the slightest movement of your hand and you had water, then just waved your hand again and paper towel was all yours. These types of places often had a curved corridor for the exit, leaving no need to touch a germy door handle.

This was the life I had gotten accustomed to when I lived in Canada.

Such a life did not exist in France. I was once discussing this with a French person who had visited Canada and they said to me, "I was shocked that everywhere we went there was a hand sanitiser mounted to the wall. What does everyone think they're going to catch?"

Fair point, my French friend.

When we moved to Paris, I quickly had to get over my fear of touching things in public, unless I wanted to go flying around the Metro at each stop for fear of touching the hand rails. Picnics in parks left me unable to wash my hands before digging into my baguette. Slowly the French way squeezed itself into my new normal.

A place like this outdoor animal park was sure to have the grossest bathrooms going. The old me wouldn't even consider stepping foot near them. But I had changed. If I could change my baby's diaper on the turned-down side of a toilet seat in a tiny Parisian bathroom, I could enter the washroom at the animal park. Also, I was pregnant and really had to pee; so I was going to find out just how bad the bathrooms were.

The old Lisa would rate these bathrooms a two on a scale from one to ten for cleanliness. The new me had a look around and deemed this place worthy of a solid six and a half. I'd definitely seen worse.

The fact of the matter was that I needed to pee and this place provided me with somewhere to do that. I was thankful. Once I'd done my business and was no longer in pee-panic mode, I took another look around and realised that maybe it was more of a five. It was outdoor, so that alone should not be allowed more than a five out of ten. But I had to give it bonus points because there was actually toilet paper, and a sink to wash my hands, with soap to boot!

The sink itself was worth taking note of. Once exiting the outdoor toilet, I was faced with a sink, that was also outside. Kevin and Océane were just on the other side of the sink watching as I finished up washing my hands. My standards of toilets in this country have been so skewed that I was just happy to have a sink and soap, never mind the dream of having them be automatic so I didn't have to touch them. As I wet my hands, I went to use the soap, but it wasn't your typical pump of *savon*. This was a solid bar of soap that had somehow been fashioned around a steel stump, mounted to the wall. The bar itself wasn't the most attractive thing I've ever laid eyes on, and it seemed to have small bits of rock or sand embedding into the bar, but it was soap nonetheless.

I wrapped my hands around the discoloured bar of soap on the metal wand beside the sink and moved them up and down, making sure I got enough soap to work up a lather. Kevin was watching me in disbelief, either because this soap system was the strangest thing he'd ever seen, or he couldn't believe I was actually touching it. It was probably a bit of both. When I was done, I looked around for paper towel but only saw a well-used old hand towel that looked like it might have been left there from last year. I decided I couldn't go that far, and shook my hands dry as I walked over to the stroller.

"Ready to go?" I asked as I bounced over, delighted to have an empty bladder.

Still in slight disbelief, Kevin broke his stare. "You've sure come a long way from the girl who wouldn't touch the handles on the Metro."

"I know, eh? Smell!" I say with the maturity of a five-year-old, as I put my freshly washed hands under his nose. "I've got the cleanest, dirty hands around!"

Baby Blunders

I had my girlfriends over to my place for coffee one morning, and Katrina and I were filling Aurelie and Mary in on our experience from the night before.

"I don't know why this town can't just have prenatal yoga classes," Katrina said. "It would be far more normal!"

"Yes, but you know the French love their swimming," Aurelie reminded us.

"Just tell us what happened!" Mary begged as she made herself at home in my kitchen, grabbing the tea and flicking on the kettle. I love when Mary does that in my house and I can just sit and relax, not really feeling like I have company over at all. If Mary walked in and I was folding laundry, she would just grab her tea and dive into folding right along with me. But we've made a deal that she won't go as far as folding Kevin's underwear 'cause that would just be weird.

"Where do I even begin to describe prenatal swimming classes?" I said to them. "Imagine a bunch of giant women in their bathing suits, and if we weren't feeling bad enough about ourselves, they of course made us all wear swim caps, so any bit of self-esteem you might have been getting from a good hair day totally disappears."

The girls nodded to show support.

"Then, as we were in the water doing leg raises, Katrina and I started having this super graphic, completely inappropriate conversation about a visit to the gyno. We were oversharing at full volume because we knew no one spoke English. Until we found out we were wrong." I looked at Katrina to take over.

"All of a sudden the woman beside me turns to me and in perfect English says, 'onto the next exercise, ladies'. We just looked at each other wanting to die. She had been listening and understood everything we were saying."

"It's like we were cheated," I told Mary and Aurelie, "If we have to live in a country where the language is a daily struggle, the least we should get is a secret language out of the deal. No one ever speaks English when you need them to. It's only when you're spilling the beans on the most graphic conversation possible that all of a sudden you've got a fluent English speaker coming out of the woodwork." I let out a sigh thinking back to the embarrassment.

"But other than that, the class was okay?" Mary asked Katrina.

"Ya, except the weird train at the end," she recalled, and we both started laughing. "You tell them," she said to me.

"Picture a bunch of pregnant women in the pool after forty-five minutes of bouncing around in the water. The instructor tells us it's time for relaxation and everyone should get one of those pool noodles. So we all grab a noodle and the instructor holds the first girl's noodle, telling her to lean back and rest her head on it, like a pillow. Then the next person puts their noodle under that girl's knees so the first girl is now totally floating. Girl number two then rests her head on the noodle that is under the first girl's knees, and puts a noodle under her own knees. We all do this, placing our noodle under the floating legs of the stranger in front of us, and then resting our head on the noodle." I started shaking my head at the memory and Katrina took over.

"It might not sound so bad, but once our heads were leaned back, we were stuck lying between a pregnant stranger's thighs. We formed this weird pregnant woman train, all lying on our backs, giant bellies in the air and the instructor pulled us around the pool for fifteen minutes. It was so weird and awkward," she told the girls.

"Weird is a nicer word than I was thinking." I smiled back at her.

"We said last night that we don't really want to go back but we've paid for the full semester, so if you need us Thursday nights, we'll be floating in the pool with our heads between some other lady's baby maker."

Katrina and I both pulled a face at the thought.

As the girls started to get ready to go pick up their kids at school, I mentioned that I was on my way for my monthly check up at the doctor.

"Say hi to Dr A for us," Aurelie joked as she put on her shoes since we all had the same gynaecologist.

When I found out I was pregnant for the second time, I didn't even entertain the idea of going back to the natural clinic. I made a bee-line to the private clinic in town; the one that wouldn't let me have a tour. I still hadn't had one, but I no longer cared. I was planning on an epidural from the first second I felt the slightest twinge in my belly. Not only did Aurelie, Katrina and I have the same gynaecologist, but in fact every English-speaking woman in the area shared this doctor, not only because he was supposed to be the best at what he did, but also because he spoke English. This obviously made things easier when talking about the health of your unborn baby. The guy had the market cornered!

"And whatever you do," Katrina shouted back as she headed to her car, "don't look in his mirror!"

"Oh my God, yes! DON'T look in his mirror!" Aurelie agreed, with a funny smile on her face.

I had no idea what that was supposed to mean, but they were both in their cars now, heading to get their kids at school, so I'd have to ask them next time.

I got in my own car and made my way to my appointment.

Once I arrived at my doctor's office, I did the standard prenatal checkup chat about how I was feeling.

Then I did the once-shocking, but now normal, half-naked weigh-in across the room from where my pants lay, followed by sauntering over to the examining table, with cellulite shimmering under the fluorescent lights. I never would have thought I'd have gotten so used to this, but it didn't seem so bad any more.

I lay back on the examining table, feet in stirrups, waiting for this awkward part of the appointment to be over, and I couldn't help but think back to Katrina and Aurelie and their voices were ringing in my ears, "Don't look in the mirror!"

Of course at lightning speed, my brain directed my eyes to do the exact opposite of my friends' advice, and almost without any say in the matter my eyes went directly to the mirror.

There were no words.

My eyes were locked and I didn't even know what to do or think. The mirror, above the sink, across from the examining table was set up on the perfect angle, giving the patient the *exact* same view that the doctor had. And you know where he was looking!

Why would they tell me to do that? Well, technically, they told me *not* to do it, but of course by saying that they knew I would. I thought back to their funny smiles in my driveway, and I was now in on their secret. I couldn't help but start laughing at the thought of telling them that I spied on the doctor checking out my pregnant pink parts in the mirror.

"*Ca va?*" The doctor asked me if I was okay as I tried to stifle my laughter. Oh man, this was embarrassing. There was dead silence in the room. I was getting an internal exam and I was laughing? Of course he was asking if I was okay. He probably thought I was crazy.

"*Oui, ca va.*" I told him I was okay, but then thinking again, about how I'd have to tell the girls about how I was so embarrassed from laughing during the check up, I started laughing again. I tried to control my giggles, but it was a vicious cycle of laughing because I shouldn't be, and thinking about telling my friends, and then laughing some more.

The doctor's eyes darted up, looking at me with a puzzled look above the frame of his glasses.

Lisa, stop laughing! This is ridiculous! I silently scolded myself.

But no amount of self-coaching could save me now. I was on a downward spiral. The more I tried not to laugh, the more I fell into a fit of nervous giggles. It was like being a pre-teen trying to hold in your laughter during an awkward sex-ed class. It was so very embarrassing and immature of me, but my body was betraying me. There was nothing I could do to end the fit of red-faced giggles I had found myself in.

Completely puzzled and probably slightly disturbed, the doctor finished my check up and made me an appointment for next time; when I would NOT be looking into that mirror. I couldn't wait to get out of there. I was going to kill Katrina and Aurelie. Or maybe just have a good laugh at my expense.

Pick up on Aisle Four

I left the world's most embarrassing appointment and instead of hunting down my friends, I thought I'd take my humiliation out on a bar of chocolate. You know, support our local economy.

Driving out to the Lindt store was great because the selection was enormous, but I knew my mom would be arriving soon for Grandma duty, so we'd go together when she got here. Instead, I would just hit the neighbourhood grocery store, and hope I didn't see the lady who thought I had one leg. Luckily I could once again stand in the pregnancy line guilt free; there was no mistaking me for just being bloated now! Once again, my baby bump was a beach ball under my shirt, instead of the standard French basketball.

As I stood in the chocolate aisle and contemplated what my treat would be, my ears perked up!

English! And not just any English, North American English!

This was hard to come by around here! There were many people living here that were from the UK, but there were five Canadians in the whole region, Kevin and I being two of them, and only a couple of Americans that lived around here.

I whipped my head around to see where the voice was coming from. It was a woman, my age, that looked nice and normal, with two young kids, and great hair.

This girl could seriously be on a Vidal Sassoon commercial with those locks!

In that moment, even though I was extremely jealous of her hair, I knew we needed to be friends. Without a moment's hesitation, I did what only an expat living in a foreign country would do.

I pushed my cart away from the chocolate (probably a blessing in disguise) and headed down the aisle, straight for her.

In my old life I never would have even entertained the idea of going up to a complete stranger in the grocery store and basically asking to be her friend. But I was living in an alternative universe where if you had a common language, it was a perfectly acceptable thing to do. I once forgot my surroundings on a visit back home and was pushing Océane through the mall, when I saw two other young moms pushing their strollers, and when I heard them speaking English I started smiling at them and actually had to stop myself from going over. But here in small-town France, there was no way I was going to stop myself from meeting a potential English-speaking friend. It was a rarity that I wasn't letting pass me by.

"You're new here, aren't you?" I asked, breaking her stare from trying to figure out what the package in her hand said.

"Yes!" She beamed. "How'd you know?"

"Because you've got an American accent and I've never seen you or your kids before... and you were staring at that box of cookies like you didn't know what it was," I joked, hoping to break the ice with my new friend-to-be.

"I'm Erica", she smiled with her overly friendly North American mannerisms that I loved instantly. "I'm from Florida and we just got here two days ago. It's all a bit overwhelming! I can't speak French and I don't even have a phone yet to do google translate."

"Nice to meet you, Erica. I'm Lisa. I know I probably seem like a stalker, but we're going to be friends, I just know it. Here's my number, call me when you get a phone and let me know what I can do to help. I've been here awhile, and my French is okay-ish, mostly."

For a quick second I thought that maybe I was being too forward. Just because I'd been here for years now, and I knew that all the English-speaking girls eventually gravitate towards each other and become friends, doesn't mean that she knew that. She was fresh off the plane, and being picked up by a pregnant lady in the grocery store probably seemed about as normal to her as the old man at the end of the aisle wearing a beret and carrying his little dog under his arm.

But my moment of uncertainty vanished as she gave me a hug, which was the most unFrench thing she could have done, and it put a huge smile on my face.

About to head back over to the chocolate, I turned back to her. "Oh, Erica, if you call and don't hear back from me, it's because I've popped." I pointed down at my belly, and we both laughed; hers likely heard from several aisles over. I added her boisterous laugh to the mental list of things I liked about my soon-to-be friend; it was second on the list, right after her Vidal Sassoon hair.

I was obviously ready to have this baby at any given moment and I bolted out of the grocery store as fast as I could, in fear it might happen right there.

And Then There Were Two

You'd think we would have learned from the first baby that we should have our parents' arrival to meet their grandchild later, rather than earlier, but I guess we were just slow learners. It was like déjà vu of waiting for Océane to be born except this time it was Kevin's parents who came first.

We were all sitting around the dinner table sweating from the heat.

"You should just go," Kevin's mom encouraged me.

"But it's so hot and I'm so huge. We'll see how I feel tomorrow... and how hot it is."

Kevin's parents had been staying with us for a couple of weeks waiting for their second grandchild, but there was still no movement. It was August and as you can imagine, an average of almost forty degrees outside with no air-conditioning felt like torture for a woman who was ready to deliver a baby.

We'd been invited to a friend's wedding. She was Scottish, he was French, and it would be my first time going to a wedding in France, so I really wanted to see what it would be like. No one thought I'd actually make it to this point without having the baby. Yet there I was, still pregnant with nothing to wear.

Mary showed up at my door what seemed like minutes after me texting her that I was thinking of just staying home because nothing fit.

"Just try this." She thrust a purple dress at me, leading me into the spare bedroom to try it on. "I wore it to a wedding when I was pregnant."

Hot and sticky, I wiggled my way into the dress.

"Mary, I look like Barney."

"What?" she called from behind the door.

"Barney. You know that giant purple dinosaur. Did you guys get that show in Scotland?"

We'd been friends for a few years now and there were still days I had a hard time understanding Mary's accent. My mom had met her several times on visits and as much as they enjoyed each other's company, there were moments when they might as well have been speaking different languages.

"Yes, I know who Barney is, and I'm sure you look nothing like him." She had a peek around the door and scoffed, "You're no Barney! Where do you come up with this stuff?"

I wiggled my way out of the dress, into my cooler sundress and headed back to everyone in the living room.

"Did you persuade her to go tomorrow?" Kevin's mom asked Mary.

As I was about to say, 'No,' Mary chimed in with, "Yes," shooting me a playfully stern look. "I'll save you guys a seat at the church tomorrow."

The next day was just as hot.

"We've got to get this baby out!" I said to Kev as we were lazing around the house. It didn't help that I was starting to feel pressure, for the second time, that our visiting family might miss the birth of their grandchild.

My in-laws went for a walk, and I was about to take a mid-day nap while Océane had hers. It was a Saturday which meant Kevin was home from work, and just as I was climbing into bed he walked into the room.

"Your parents are going to fly back before the baby even arrives," I moaned.

"I'm worried you might be right. It's getting close."

"You remember what the doctor 'prescribed' with Océane?" I said with a coy smile.

"Italian induction?"

I nodded, raising my eyebrows twice for effect.

"No way, my parents will be home any second!" he weakly protested.

"So what, pretend you're a teenager. This baby needs to be born."

We made our way downstairs awhile later wearing our poker faces when we greeted our house guests. It was like we were waiting for a timer to go off, as if I would magically go into labour moments later. No such luck. A few hours had passed and there were still no signs of baby movement.

"I'm going to take another shower," I announced, exiting the room. "I guess I'll get to go to my first French wedding after all."

We walked into the church and as promised, Mary saved us a spot. On the way over I sent her a request by text that if she was saving a seat for us, it needed to be at the very back of the church. If this baby did come, I needed a quick exit. There was no way I was stealing the show.

"Where's the Barney dress?" Mary whispered as I scooted in beside her. I gave Mary *la bise,* but in a very unFrench way, I refused to go around double-kissing everyone else who wasn't beside me. It was too hot and I was too big, so I simply blew a couple of quick kisses to Aurelie and Katrina and sent a few waves to their husbands. I was sitting on the Scottish side of the church so I was sure I'd be forgiven.

"It was too Barney. Kev agreed. I thought I'd go black, I hear it's slimming." And we both giggled, knowing black was no help to me now.

The wedding was lovely, and I made it through unnoticed, until it was time for communion. I couldn't help but notice a few whispers as I passed the aisles. I wondered if people were placing bets.

My friend, the bride, was as kind as she was beautiful, and when she heard that I shared my due date with her wedding date, she completely understood that there was only a fifty percent chance I'd be showing up. When I made my way to the front of the church, I loved that her eyes, and her smile, grew as big as my belly when she saw me coming down the aisle baby first, taking up more than my share of space in the line. Back of the church or not, there was no hiding me now.

Once again I was carrying this baby in a very unFrenchly way with my enormous belly. As I returned to the back of the church and passed the French side of the wedding, eyes grew, just as the bride's had. I was definitely in full bloom.

Eyes front, people, look at the bride, there's nothing to see here.

After the ceremony we made our way to the nearby chateau about twenty minutes from the church. Without meaning to, I caught myself making a mental note that we were now forty minutes from home, no hospital bag in the car, and I was forty weeks pregnant to the day. But it was a flickering thought and I carried on, wanting to enjoy the party.

It was a lovely mix-up of cultures, as many of our friends were. The bride's Scottish side was represented with bagpipes and when they were done the older men in *berets* sauntered in singing old Basque tunes in barbershop quartet-style, accompanied by accordions.

"Now this is a wedding!" I said to Kevin as we made our way to check out the mountain of food and drinks set up in the outdoor tent. "Actually," I paused, "get yourself a drink, I'm just going to run to the bathroom."

"Okay, I'll get you a Perrier."

I left Kevin chatting away with our friends as I made my way into the chateau to find the bathroom.

I felt a twinge, but passed it off as gas or something. I went to the bathroom and nothing irregular happened, but I couldn't help but feel a little 'off'. I walked back out to the vineyard and felt another little twinge in my abdomen.

I didn't really know what going into labour normally felt like because I was induced with Océane, so a year and a half earlier, I went from nothing, to being hit by a transport truck in five seconds. I knew I wasn't anywhere near active labour but all I couldn't help but think of was this afternoon's 'Italian Induction' and how there was no way in hell I wanted my water to break in Hollywood-movie-fashion at my friend's wedding.

I went back over to the group and stood a little extra close to Kevin to get his attention.

Are you okay? he asked me by simply raising his eyebrows.

"I think maybe we should start saying goodbye to everyone. But keep it cool. I don't want a scene."

His eyes got bright and a smile smeared across his face. He took me by the hand, and we did a lightning-fast round of goodbyes before we buckled up and Kevin peeled out of that chateau as if we had stolen something.

I lost track of how many times he asked if I was okay on the ride home. I still wasn't having contractions, but I was definitely having stomach pains, and stomach pains at forty weeks pregnant, after the Italian Induction, meant that there was likely a baby coming in our not-so-distant future.

As we drove the forty minutes from the chateau back into town, the stomach pains turned to cramping, and I knew we'd be making a trip to the hospital soon.

I tried to make small talk and visit with Kevin's parents a bit when we got home, but that didn't last more than a few minutes.

"I'm going to head to bed. Kev, you might not want to stay up too late. I have a feeling tonight might be a long night."

My feeling was right. Kevin had slipped into bed without me noticing, and a few hours later we were awoken by the Atlantic unleashing itself on our bed.

"OHMYGOD GROSS!" I shouted as I jumped out of bed.

"It's go-time!" Kevin announced as if he had just had seventy-two cups of coffee. He grabbed my bag, threw it in the trunk, and pulled the car up to the front door before I even moved from the spot I was standing. I grabbed one of Océane's diapers to dam the flood of the Atlantic and waddled down the stairs.

We made it to the hospital in record time, whereupon entering the building, I announced to whoever was listening that I was ready for an epidural.

I didn't know a lot of medical terms in French, but I made damn sure that I knew how to say that line. The fact that I wasn't even completely through the maternity doors yet meant that I was requesting the epidural from the first person dressed like they had some kind of connection to the hospital. For all I knew she could have been part of the cleaning staff and not a medical professional in the least, but I didn't really care. I just didn't want to relive my first labour and delivery.

"Are you experiencing pain?" the lady wearing scrubs asked in French.

"Not really, I just want to be ready." By the look she gave me, I could tell they weren't used to pregnant foreigners cracking jokes in the middle of the night as they arrived at the labour and delivery entrance.

My doctor with the terribly situated mirror was very kind and understood my anxiety, so it was actually written in my chart that I wanted the epidural and at no time should it be turned off, or down.

A nurse came over to get me and ensured me that she would take good care of me. She told Kevin that she was just going to give me a quick examination to see how far along I was before we went straight to the epidural.

One centimetre.

I was only one centimetre dilated and even I wanted to laugh at the idea that I had already asked for an epidural. Maybe it was a bit premature after all. But we were still in France and they aren't in the business of turning people away from hospitals. She got us a room, got us settled in and that would be our home base until the baby was born.

When it eventually was time for the epidural, I wanted to go back in time twenty-two months and smack my old self for trying to be tough. I was instantly relieved of pain, and Kevin and I just hung out for a few hours, instead of him rubbing my back while I moaned like a mammoth beast as I got in and out of the tub searching for the slightest bit of relief.

This time my experience was unbelievable. Since it was night time in France, that meant that my family was all awake in Canada. High on epidural-love, we were sending them pictures from the delivery room, Kevin with scrubs and me in my sexy hospital gown.

Everything was going amazingly until the nurses had their shift change.

The new nurse came in and introduced herself to us. As soon as she heard my accent speaking French, she knew I wasn't local. She started firing questions at me in French.

Where are you from? Do you have family here? It must be hard to have a baby so far from home and in a language that isn't your own. You must miss your family. Too bad they're so far away. It must be a really difficult time for you.

Nice to meet you too, Debbie Downer! I was actually doing just fine until you came around and starting messing with my hormonal emotions. Note to self: never start pointing out all the negative aspects of a person's life to them when they are lacking sleep and their body is exuding high levels of labour hormones. My eyes started welling up with tears, and Kevin glared at this woman like he might exude physical harm upon her. In his perfect French, he cut off her questioning and told her that I'm amazing, tough, strong and that he couldn't be more proud of me. Which, of course, made me cry even more. *Take that, nurse.* I was rescued by my knight in shining blue hospital scrubs.

"Thanks," I whispered to him in English. "Shame about the shift change." And with a giggle I wiped my tears and was back to my old self, happy for the secret language we had between us in the delivery room.

In hindsight she was only trying to be nice, but it was not the time or the place for her emotion-inducing line of questioning.

I think I probably scared my doctor with all the post-traumatic stress disorder stories that I had from my attempt at natural childbirth because he didn't even suggest that I push until it was really REALLY time for that baby to be born. I basically sneezed. I couldn't believe this was the same thing happening. I had had trips to the dentist that were more painful than delivering my second baby.

By barely breaking a sweat, a new baby was placed on my chest. I knew now that I must be becoming bilingual, because we waited to find out the sex of the baby, and I have no recollection of which language they told me in, but I had had another sweet baby girl.

We were hit by the love-truck once again, and words could not describe it.

Elodie. We were blessed with another French princess, and her name would be Elodie.

Hospital Food

I gave birth to Océane in a public, government-run French maternity hospital. Elodie was born in a private clinic less than two years later. This allowed me to feel like I was fairly well informed on the health care system, at least for a foreigner, because I had experienced both, first hand, in a rather short time.

The public hospital, in some ways provided me with more than the private hospital actually did. The only thing they told me to bring was an outfit to bring my baby home in. They provided everything else I needed: diapers, creams, soaps, baby clothes, towels and blankets until the moment I walked out the door. In the private hospital they asked me to bring those things from home, which wasn't a big deal. It just meant packing a bigger bag.

There were several things that were consistent across both hospitals. The first being the length of my stay. It is standard practice in France to stay in the hospital for a minimum of four to five days, if you've had a regular birth with no complications. If you're thinking it's a money grab, you are mistaken, because it's covered, which was normal for me coming from the Canadian healthcare system.

When I had Océane I had clearly never breastfed before. There was a call button beside my bed that I was instructed to press every time I wanted to feed my baby and instantly a lactation consultant would arrive at my bedside helping me the first few times, and making sure the baby was latching correctly after that. I stopped using the button after the first day, but they kept telling me I should be using it the whole time I was there. I didn't have any breastfeeding issues (besides being a nervous wreck feeding in small Parisian cafés) but I can imagine this would be great for new moms that struggled.

My first experience also had a nurse come to my room daily and help bathe our new baby, which was great because newborns are slippery little suckers. They showed us everything from water temperature, through to cleaning our new babies nose and ears. It was like being in a hands-on parenting class. It wasn't necessary when Elodie was born, because we were obviously professionals by then, but I felt really grateful when Océane arrived because it eased the deer-in-the-headlights look that both Kevin and I were sporting as new parents.

The best feature that both hospitals had, by far, was the food. I should have known the French wouldn't mess around with cuisine, even in the hospital. Each morning someone would come in with a tablet and take my order for the upcoming day. Every meal had several choices and with Océane the French still intimidated me, so I always jumped on the *poulet* option whenever I heard it. I figured I'd always be safe with chicken.

During Elodie's hospital stay, I was feeling a bit more confident with my French and got adventurous with my orders. Sometimes I'd try the fish, other times I'd have steak or French-style casseroles. God knows I was in there long enough to test out a few different meal options.

"Do you want me to order something for you for dinner?" I asked Kevin as he packed up a bag.

For both of the girls' births he took a couple of weeks off work (standard French jobs give nine weeks holidays, so he had a few weeks he could spare) and both times he stayed at the hospital with me, keeping me company. With Elodie's birth he was close enough to home that he could go home to drop off our laundry for my mother-in-law who was holding down the fort. He would pick up Océane and bring her to visit her new sister, whom she loved because she thought she was a baby doll come to life, then he'd drop her back at home to spend time with her grandparents, and Kevin would make his way back to me at the hospital for dinner. Only in France do you purposely go out of your way to eat hospital food.

Also, in the hospital was the only time I found dinner served at eighteen hours thirty.

"C'est tot," the person taking my order warned me that they'd be serving dinner 'early', but six thirty p.m. was just fine with me.

When meal time came, I put Elodie in the basinette beside my bed and started to wiggle my way out of bed.

"I'll get it," Kevin offered, trying to stop me from getting up.

"Are you kidding? This is a highlight of the day," and by this time I had been there several days and was feeling fine, really.

I waddled myself to the door of my room where there was a cute little food stand that looked like a brasserie to go and was far too posh for a hospital. Behind the food cart stood a gentleman in a tall chef's hat, ready to make my French food dreams come true.

"Bonsoir, madame!" he chirped in a sing-song voice, thoroughly enjoying his job. *"Qu'est-ce que vous voulez choisir ce soir?"* He asked what I had chosen, and I informed him I'd be having the veal.

Imagine how you might picture the stereotypical 'hospital food' slopped onto a plate, and now picture the complete opposite.

The chef carefully arranged a fresh salad with crisp vegetables on a small plate and topped it with two small toasts covered in warm goat cheese, drizzled with honey. The *salade chèvre chaud* would have been enough to keep me happy, but that was just the first course. We were in France, there was always at least three courses!

Next he plated the veal, drizzling an au jus on top, accompanied by roasted baby potatoes and steamed vegetables. He then cut off an extra large slice of warm baguette. "*C'est pour le bébé.*" He winked when he saw my eyes get big at the extra large portion of bread.

He placed my baguette on a side plate next to another large portion, this time, of camembert. He must have known the way to my heart was through my stomach!

The cheese course was for after the meal, but before dessert. I now had that French rule down to a science.

He then made room on my tray for a glass dish of *mousse au chocolat,* just what the doctor ordered to finish off this restaurant worthy meal. He arranged my tray, just so, clearly taking pride in his art, offered me a Perrier, and passed me my tray, wishing me, *"Bon Appétit".*

"This is the best hospital food ever," I said to Kevin as we sat in the corner of the room having a romantic little dinner for two.

"It sure is," he agreed in between bites of his very rare *côte de boeuf.*

As good as the food was, the walls of the hospital room were closing in on me, and I was ready to get back home so we could be together as a family.

When Océane was born, I lost a lot of blood and ended up fainting several times after I was back in my room, so they kept a close eye on me, and I had several iron transfusions before I was back on my feet. They only moved me around by wheelchair when it was time to bath Océane the first few days, but even then, by day five I was really ready to go home. Trying to sign myself out was almost like breaking out of prison.

I was starting to find that you need to be in top form, skipping around your room for them to feel you're fit to leave.

"J'ai pense vraiment que je suis prête!" I tried to convince the nurse that I really thought I was ready to go home.

It had been four days since Elodie was born and I was really missing Océane. She'd come and see me every day, but I missed waking up to her, and putting her to sleep. I wanted our life as a new family to begin.

I knew what I had to do to bust myself out of the hospital. Like I said before, I was somewhat of a professional at this now. I was ready to pull out the big guns. They wouldn't be able to say no.

"Je ferai un rendez-vous avec la sage-femme." I told the nurse that I would make an appointment with the midwife, and I knew that would make her let me out. It's the only way they would let me leave 'early' when Océane was born. Yes, they considered me asking to leave on day four, early.

"Pfffff." The nurse let out a big puff of air, in typical French fashion when they are showing exasperation or admitting defeat. She was displaying both, and I glanced at Kevin, beaming because I knew I was going home.

With assurance that a midwife would come to my house to check on me in the morning (and several appointments following that), my doctor scratched his signature on my release form, and I was a free woman.

I missed the food, and not having to do any house work, but I was ready to go home and be in my own house.

Scary Stuff

In hindsight, I should have appreciated the quiet of the hospital while I had it, because nothing really prepared me for the chaos of balancing two kids under two years old for the first time.

When I brought Océane home from the hospital, it was all snuggles (and crying), mid-afternoon naps and gazing into each other's eyes.

Bringing Elodie home from the hospital, I learned the skill of breastfeeding while chasing a toddler around the house, ensuring she didn't impale herself on the corner of a table. We were blessed with not just one, but a second colicky, and/or reflux baby, so once again there was a lot of crying. Gone were the days of napping in the lounge chair with my newborn on my chest. Those were replaced by beautiful chaos, and a period of my life in a blur of constant motion.

In my mind Océane wasn't anywhere near going to school. She was barely two years old, but in France school starts young. As soon as kids are potty trained, they start *Petite Section,* meaning there's little two-and-a half-year-olds in school; this is something that both the teacher and the mom in me had a hard time imagining.

It was already the middle of October, but the month seemed to have snuck up on me. I didn't realise it was nearly Halloween until I was talking to my brother on the computer and his kids came barrelling into the room, dying to show me their Halloween costumes.

"I miss Halloween," I told my brother once the kids scurried out of the room. "Although I probably save myself three pounds and a few zits by not celebrating it any more."

"You'll probably get zits anyway," countered my brother in the child-like banter we still carried into adulthood.

I wrapped up the conversation with my brother and headed outside to check the mail. I smiled as the sun shone down on me and it still felt like summer, even though we were well into fall.

There was an invitation for Océane in the mailbox. I flipped it over to find that she had been invited to the school Halloween party so she could get to know some of the kids and teachers before her possible start in January.

January?

I was double shocked. She was way too young to be starting school in January. Whether we lived in France or not, it wasn't happening on my watch. She would at least wait until the following September because even then, she would still be under three years old and perhaps I'd warm up to the idea with time. The greater shock might have been that there was going to be a Halloween party? I couldn't believe it! I needed to check it out. We would definitely be there; French people don't do Halloween, so this would be interesting.

It's not that Halloween didn't exist in France. It was slowly starting to creep into stores, but it wasn't anywhere near the scale of what it was at home.

When I first moved to Paris, I was told flat out that they didn't celebrate Halloween in France. And for the most part, that was true. I saw no sign of it in any stores no matter how hard I looked for those mini-chocolate bars. So I gave up, and accepted the fact that it indeed did not happen in France.

Imagine the shock, and panic I faced on October thirty-first when I heard a knock on my door and two somewhat costumed teenagers stood in front of me holding open bags, waiting for candy. Those poor trailblazing Parisian trick or treaters ended up with a granola bar and a pack of gum each. I was horrified to think that I may have missed the memo, but it turns out that those two kids were just ahead of the curve, bringing the tradition of Halloween to a country that didn't know they were arriving.

Of course the next year I was ready, with chocolate bars piled on my counter and not a single knock at the door. Go figure.

Since Océane was born we celebrated Halloween with other foreign families in our anglophone playgroup. The kids would wear costumes, we'd have some Halloween-themed snacks and that would be it.

Not exactly the Halloween I had as a kid, but it was better than nothing.

With a Tiger costume imported from the Disney store in Canada, and a tiny, crying baby dinosaur bundled up in the stroller, we were all set to check out what this school had planned for Halloween.

As we arrived I realised that the 'foreigner' sign must have been brightly flashing above our heads, yet again. Apparently we didn't get the memo that in France everyone is a zombie, or a witch for Halloween. No princesses, or superheros, no doctors, and definitely no Tiger or dinosaurs. Only witches and zombies. *Mental note for next year.*

The head of the parent council had all the kids and their parents waiting in the school yard at four p.m. It turns out this was not a school event, but a parent council event because school was on one of their many holidays. A few quick instructions rattled off in immensely rapid-fire French and they were off. The kids took to the street parade-style through the neighbourhood chanting, "*On veut des bonbons! On veut des bonbons!*" 'We want candy' doesn't seem like the most polite thing to shout in the face of the person giving you said candy, but this is what French kids say in place of 'trick or treat'.

Flyers were delivered to the houses where kids would be coming. The houses that responded to the flyer were waiting with candy in hand, and then suddenly were bombarded with all the kids at once, creating slight pandemonium. The houses that hadn't noticed the flyer in their mailbox informing them of these happenings were clearly surprised. But the excitement of the children was contagious, and elderly French ladies with no clue of what this 'Halloween' event was, came running out to the street with boxes of cookies and tins of mints, whatever they could get their hands on, just as I did that first Halloween in Paris.

Since the stores weren't set up with the mini-chocolate bars and small bags of chips to hand out to trick or treaters, the things going into Océane's little bag were alarming from a Canadian standpoint. After the first house, she followed all the kids to the next stop, and I had a peek in her bag. I actually gasped out loud. *Unwrapped candy!*

Growing up, we were always taught not to eat anything until our parents had checked it, and by no means were you to ever eat unwrapped candy. Yet here I was, in a country that was new to Halloween, where they didn't know about the rules that were drilled into my head as a child. Instead, they opened bags of gummy bears and tossed them into the kids' bags by the handful. Boxes of cookies were opened and passed out, one per child. And what as a child I called five-cent candies, were loosely placed into trick or treaters' bags.

The kids happily walked down the street eating the unwrapped candy as they went, parents happily watching, as if they weren't breaking the number one rule of North American trick or treating.

I couldn't stop myself from texting Kevin at work.

"They're giving out unwrapped candy, and all the parents are letting their kids eat it. It's like I'm in the twilight zone, again."

"Relax, Lis. Small town. They don't know Halloween. Let her eat the candy, or you'll be the weird one."

He was right. I was in a world different from my own; I needed to use the other parents as a gauge. It was a good neighbourhood. These people loved their kids, and I was just being a bit neurotic. But mostly because I was in shock by the fact that we were all breaking the cardinal rule of Halloween. I took a deep breath and said, 'of course' with a smile when Océane asked if she could eat the cookie floating in her little bag.

The *boulangerie* even took part by making ghost-shaped meringues for each child. Once again I had a fleeting thought of, 'unwrapped candy!', but after I jumped the first hurdle, the rest were easy after that. I knew things are always more relaxed around here than I was used to, but sometimes it still caught me off guard.

Océane had the time of her life. Running through the streets, wearing a costume, demanding candy… and people actually gave it to her! She didn't care if there were no jack-o-lanterns and there were only twenty kids trick or treating, opposed to the two-hundred running through her cousins' suburban neighbourhood in Canada. She still had genuine fun, unwrapped candy and all!

La Toussaint

I did love our little village, as sleepy as it was. We were only about fifteen minutes from Pau's city centre, which we referred to as our 'downtown'. Apart from that, it was just one little village that ran into the next, each with its own tiny community.

Sometimes I envied my friends' slightly larger, yet still tiny, villages because they had a restaurant, a pharmacy or a brasserie. Ours was too small for that, but if I needed any of those things, they were just a few minutes away.

Even if our neighbourhood was pretty sleepy, it would still surprise me every so often. Like the day after Halloween when I was driving along, minding my own business and suddenly was stopped in my tracks.

I was driving past the school and caught something out of the corner of my eye that caused me to slam on my brakes. I don't know why I'd never noticed before that just up from the school, beside the church, there was a cemetery.

As the brakes stopped the car, my karaoke session with the French radio station came to a halt and I pulled over to the side of the road. If any neighbours were watching I'm sure they were wondering what the token foreigner was doing now. As it was, the French were starting to bundle up with jackets and hats, but there I was, no jacket in November, car pulled over, and now standing mesmerised in the middle of the village cemetery.

It's not that I'm a stranger to cemeteries. As a kid, every spring my mom would drag my brothers and I to plant flowers at the graves of relatives that had passed away. My older brothers would scare me by chasing me through the cemetery, and my mom would end up planting the flowers herself, but it still meant that I was no stranger to cemeteries.

This cemetery, however, had me in awe. The amount of fresh, bright, beautiful flowers that covered this patch of land was completely impressive! There wasn't a single gravestone that wasn't covered with an immaculate assortment of fresh flowers. I'd never seen anything like it. It was the prettiest, most magazine-worthy cemetery I've ever come across.

I needed an explanation. So I did as I always do when I'm thrown, amazed, or shocked by life in France: I called Kevin at work.

After rambling incessantly in his ear about how I'm standing amongst all these amazing flowers, he finally managed to squeeze in a couple of puzzled words. "Why are you at a cemetery?"

I explained to him that it looked like a botanical garden and it caught my eye from the road, and so I pulled over the car and got out.

"Ask around and see if anybody knows what this is all about and let me know later," I requested before hanging up.

Of course I had no patience to wait, so from there in the cemetery I decided to call Coco. She was French and she lived in this village so maybe she would know. As the phone started ringing, I quickly realised that I didn't know the French word for cemetery because, thankfully, it doesn't usually come up in conversation.

"*Bonjour, Lisa! Ca va?*"

We exchanged the standard pleasantries and then, still not knowing the proper word for cemetery I tried to figure out what was going on while speaking French, but my words ended up coming out sounding like this:

"I'm just across from the school, at the place where the dead people are. I don't know the name for it in French. There are flowers everywhere. Why? Who did this? It's so pretty this place for the dead people."

Since Coco had now been our neighbour for years, and she had a big hand in me learning French from our daily conversations, thankfully, she didn't even break stride at my strange wording. Like Kevin though, she was slightly amused that I was randomly calling her from the cemetery.

Coco explained to me that November first is *La Toussaint*, All Saints Day. It's a holiday in France, and that much I knew because everything was closed. What I didn't know was that French people pay tribute to their relatives and loved ones that have passed away by visiting the cemetery, completely transforming it by putting fresh flowers everywhere. There wasn't a single grave missed. Flowers flooded the headstones, and Coco told me that chrysanthemums were the traditional favourite, and the French love tradition.

When I heard back from Kevin, I had already left the cemetery, but we confirmed that our stories matched. Which led me to my next question. "Do you think they'd let me be buried here one day?"

I could feel Kevin rolling his eyes through the phone, but I was kind of serious. You've got to hand it to the French for once again not messing around! They unfailingly stick to tradition and leave foreigners like myself in disbelieving amazement.

It was easily the loveliest cemetery I've set eyes on. If there was a cemetery that was decked out in diamonds, stilettos, and a glass of champagne in hand; this was it! And for the first time ever, I wished that this place 'where dead people were buried' was in my backyard.

The Revolving Door

The problem with having so many of your friends being part of the international community is that many of us are transient. We were a perfect example. We had been sent to France through Kevin's company, but we didn't really know how long they were going to keep us there. Lucky enough, we'd been in France quite a few years, with no sign of moving, so we just kept our heads down and hoped that Kevin's company would forget we were even here. If they would have let us stay until retirement, we would have taken them up on that.

My friends, however, knew their days were numbered. For some reason that particular year there was a mass exodus of foreigners, and a good chunk being some of my closest friends.

"Who's going to drive me to all the parties now?" I said to Aurelie, half-joking over morning coffee when she told me she was going to leave.

"And you too!" I was now ribbing Katrina, who was on her way back to Australia. "I'm going to have to sweep my own floor after playgroup and that's really gonna suck."

I was making light of the situation, but was actually feeling quite sad. These girls had really been there for me, welcoming me in from the moment I arrived, through our matching pregnancies, and into round two of playgroup with our newest babies.

"Why are you so glum?" Kevin asked as I was preparing dinner that night. "Tough day at the office with the little ladies?"

The fact that Elodie was rounding her third month of crying didn't help matters, but to be honest, I kinda felt like I wanted to join her.

"All my friends are moving," I moped. "Mary will still be here, but there's a whack of people leaving this year, including Aurelie and Katrina."

"Well, I've got just the news you need to hear then," he said, picking up Océane and lifting her to my cheek in an attempt to cheer me up while I cooked dinner.

"Donne un bisou à *Maman."* He told her to give me a kiss, and she did, instantly cheering me up, as he knew it would.

Having French spoken in the house was normal now, and was really helping me with my French as well. Kevin spoke French at home growing up, and didn't really speak much English until he was a teenager. Then when he decided to go to university in English, he became perfectly bilingual, making it almost impossible to hear an accent on him in either language. He and I always spoke English together but when the girls were born, he wanted them to have both languages, which was important for us as Canadians, but even more so since we lived in France.

From the first moment he held them in the hospital room, he's only spoken French to them and I've only spoken English, not wanting them picking up my French grammar. Océane, from the moment she could talk, began speaking both languages, responding appropriately in whichever language she was addressed. This was amazing to me, who still struggled after all these years.

Kevin, being the stickler that he was, told Océane when Elodie came home from the hospital, that her new sister spoke French. I gave him a sideways glance but couldn't help but smirk when, without missing a beat, Océane leaned into the car seat and gave her new sister a little "Bonjour EE", because when the three syllables of 'Elodie' is too hard for a toddler to pronounce, it got cut to EE.

"What's your news then?" I asked, trying to hide my smile even though he already knew that Océane's *bisou* had lifted my spirit.

"There's Canadians moving here!"

"What!" I spun around. "Who? When? How do you know?"

"Calm down," he laughed, grabbing some plates from the cupboard and bringing them over to the table.

"Do you remember Joel from Calgary? He moved there just before we left, but I actually went to school with him on the east coast?"

This sounded vaguely familiar, but really, I hadn't had a good night's sleep in two years. I couldn't even remember what I had for breakfast, never mind someone that I'd never met, who my husband went to school with a decade ago, before we even knew each other.

"He and I went golfing the week before we left Canada, then he came over and we couldn't even offer him a glass for his beer because they were all packed."

Maybe this was ringing a bell after all.

"Anyway, they're moving here soon, and they have a son who is just a few months older than Océane."

"How's his wife? Nice? Weird? Will I like her?" I was so hopeful, pleading for any information he could give me. Canadians were so few and far between, and I was always envious of the Scottish girls and how many of them there were. All I could do is hope that I'd hit it off with Joel's wife and have a maple-syrup-sister in the south of France.

"I've never met her, but I'll invite them over as soon as they get here." He smiled, seeing my excitement.

"Of course!" I brought dinner to the table and had a little spring in my step for the rest of the evening.

***

It was officially moving season and goodbye parties were in full swing. Mary, Aurelie, Katrina and I used that as a perfect excuse to escape for a girls' weekend. It was my first time leaving Elodie over night, but I knew Kevin could handle it, and I couldn't pass up a weekend in Epernay, which was the heart of Champagne region in France.

We took the one-hour flight to Paris, then armed with Champagne to get us ready, we popped the bottle on the one-hour train ride to get from Paris to the Champagne region. Two friends that had recently moved to Paris hopped on a train and met us there for the weekend. It was one of those magical places that you couldn't live in France without visiting, or at least that's how I sold it to Kevin.

For us girls, it was a chance to have some much needed grown-up time, eat great food and drink fabulous Champagne. We did a few tours, like the Moet and Dom Perignon caves, which had us nearly tasting Champagne for breakfast, but we weren't complaining.

After all the excitement of the weekend, I came home feeling a bit like I needed a vacation from my vacation. I never went out late-night drinking any more, let alone two nights in a row. The only reason I'd been up late in the past two years was to feed a baby, and my body was feeling the pain.

"You must've had a good time, because you're looking pretty tired," Kevin joked as I walked through the front door.

I dropped my bag, opened my arms and soaked up all the cuddles I'd missed over the weekend as Océane tackled me at the door. With her on my hip, I spread the love to the rest of my family, then hit the couch to give Kevin the debrief of the weekend.

When I was finally done, he spoke up. "I'm got a little news myself." He coyly raised an eyebrow.

"Out with it!"

"Joel and Jaclyn will be here this week."

I could see he was proud to be the one delivering me this news but I was drawing a blank.

"... Joel and Jaclyn?" I gave him a pleading face, hoping for a clue.

"The Canadians!"

"Oh, right! That's fantastic." I genuinely was happy about the news, but I was just a bit too tired to give him the full enthusiasm he had anticipated.

He let me know that him and Joel would work out a plan for us all to get together.

"Sounds good. Don't forget to pass along my number, and tell Joel that Jaclyn can call anytime she needs something." I suddenly realised that I was now filling the role that Aurelie had played for me upon my arrival, and it became clear to me that I wasn't being a pain or an inconvenience back then. English speakers living in France were genuinely happy to welcome new potential friends. There were so few of us in the area that us foreigners had to stick together. The idea of a Canadian calling me was the opposite of inconvenient; it was exciting!

A few days later I got a midday call from Kevin. "How's tomorrow to have Joel and his family over? Canada is playing, it'll be great."

The Olympics were on and by 'playing' I knew he meant hockey.

"Sounds good, I'll run out and pick up a few things."

Océane really didn't have that long in the front seat of the grocery cart until Elodie was out of the baby carrier and into that spot. But she didn't seem to mind because she was happy to hang out in the actual wagon part. Unfortunately for me, that meant that anything I actually put into the cart would likely be sat on by a toddler. Toilet paper and six-pack cans of Perrier, not a problem, but bags of chips that I wanted for our little party with our new Canadian friends, well, that was a different story.

I was actually really excited to have them over because my 'casual Canadian party' excuse would be legit this time.

I made a taco dip, a pizza, veggies and dip and bought some chicken wings. It was all perfect food for watching an Olympic hockey game, and all very unFrench since it all had to be eaten with our hands. But because we'd been in France for several years, it had seeped into our everyday, and I couldn't have people over without also having some cut-up baguette, slicing some *saucisson*, which was a delicious, locally made dried sausage and, of course, I had a wheel of camembert on hand in case we wanted to throw in on the BBQ later.

There was beer, wine and Champagne in the outside fridge, because no matter how long we'd been in France, I still over shopped and, in true North American fashion, we had a backup fridge. Ours was just through the kitchen in the attached garage (aka Kevin's gym and our laundry room). It was always stocked with a plethora of beverages in case the mood struck.

Not long after Kevin was finished work, the newest Canadians to the region had arrived. They didn't stand out at the street and ring the bell at the gate of the house before even thinking of entering the property, like a French person most definitely would. Instead, they strolled right up the driveway, skipped the bell and knocked on the door like we were old friends. Technically speaking, Kevin and Joel *were* old friends from university, so I suppose that changed things, but they were both new friends to me.

Océane went running for the door as soon as she found out a little playmate would be on the other side. The kids were off and running, two peas in a pod from the moment they met. This was going to be good.

I did a quick assessment of our fellow Canadians. Joel looked vaguely familiar which meant Kevin was right and I had met him years ago, right before we left for France. Much to my delight, Jaclyn seemed perfectly normal. I'm not sure what I was expecting, but I suppose subconsciously I wasn't letting myself get my hopes up.

"We brought beer," they announced as they walked in. "And I brought my slippers," Jaclyn shyly announced under her breath, sort of laughing at herself.

Quirky; I liked her already. This was going to work out just fine. We spent the rest of the day eating, drinking, and watching the kids play.

My Canadian-style snacks were warmly received, and no one in the room had any sort of issue eating with their hands. There was something really comfortable about there being no language, or even accent barrier and having no cultural blocking points. It was as if we had known these guys for ages, and again, Kevin actually had, but now I was on board too, and I couldn't be happier.

As they were on their way out, I remembered that there was a girls' night out the following evening.

"Jaclyn, before you go." I stopped her as she was leaving. "Tomorrow night is Karina's leaving party. I know you don't know her, but it really doesn't matter, everyone will be there. You should come. We'll go together."

And just like that I officially had become a less punctual version of Aurelie. It seemed like ages ago that I met my now very close friend, and she invited me to a leaving party the very next day after I met her. It was where I met a room full of women who welcomed me in to my new home, making all the difference in the world to a new girl in a foreign land. And now there I was, the veteran, bringing in the new girl, assuring her she would be welcome at the party of someone she'd never met.

She accepted my offer, and I had a new friend.

And so continued the revolving door of foreign friends in our little French town.

The Newbies

I picked Jaclyn up by taxi at the awful apartment-hotel that we also got placed in on our arrival. I was twenty minutes later than Aurelie would have been, but she didn't seem to mind.

As we drove, each with a bottle of wine beside us, resting on the middle seat between us in the back of the taxi, and me with my famous taco dip on my lap, I debriefed her on who the party was for, whose house it was at, and who would be there. These descriptions mainly consisted of which country these girls were from and how long they had lived here. Sometimes what country a person came from was added in, or what country they were moving to. I basically kept track of people with a geographical map of the world in my mind. It may seem strange, but when your friends and acquaintances hailed from all corners of the earth, it did the trick.

We walked into the party, and now Jaclyn understood a bit better what I meant. There were women there from Ireland, Scotland, Australia, Nigeria, England, Indonesia, Germany, Venezuela, and as of that moment, Canada. I was so happy to have a sister of the maple leaf with me.

There was one country I left out because I didn't spot her there right away. She hadn't turned around yet, but I knew it was Vidal Sassoon by those beautiful locks of hair.

"Florida, right?" I asked when she turned around.

"Yes!" she said, beaming. It took her a second, and then a light bulb went off while she looked me up and down. "You're the pregnant grocery store girl!"

"Indeed I am, but pregnant no more!" And I clinked her glass with the one Katrina magically made appear in my hand at the perfect moment. Vidal Sassoon reminded me that her name was actually Erica. She lost my number in the move-in process, and I forgot about our meeting, you know, with having a baby and all. But the town was small, and of course it was only a matter of time before our paths crossed in the circle of English-speaking moms.

Amongst the foreigners, one thing we all had in common was our struggle with French. With Aurelie having gone, I had moved into the top spot of best French speaker in our group and for that I couldn't be prouder. It wasn't uncommon for someone to call and ask me to phone and make a doctor's appointment for them, or if there was a group dinner, I was always nominated to call and make the reservation. I had Coco to thank, and the chatter of my husband with our kids in the house, buzzing in my ears. The French language had finally seeped into my brain. It still wasn't perfect, but it did the trick.

Erica's kids went to the International School, so she quickly found herself swept up in the English-speaking mom circle, many of which were the ladies who formerly attended play group with me, so our mutual friends overlapped nicely.

"Oh my God, taco dip is my favourite!" Erica announced in her natural over-excited way, revealing that she shared North American roots both in accent and tastebuds. Although Katrina had snuck by to place a glass of Champagne in my right hand, I was still balancing a taco dip in my left, as Erica had pointed out.

I excused myself and went to place the food on the coffee table, peeking over my shoulder to see if Jaclyn was okay. I got sidetracked by the excitement of re-meeting Erica at the door, but the joy of this group was that no one was strangers for long. Jaclyn was busy being chatted up by several different women. She was the new girl after all; people wanted to know her story!

When Jaclyn and I crossed paths again a short time later, she was the one introducing me to someone new.

"Have you met Beth?" she asked, adding, "She's also new," as an unnecessary explanation as to why she knew her and I didn't.

"Hi, Beth, nice to meet you," and we did the obligatory two-cheeked bisous, even though neither of us were French.

Beth was gorgeous, and I wondered if she was in France on some kind of modelling stint in Paris. She had a British accent, perfect makeup and fantastic hair. She just oozed cool, almost to the point of intimidation. When I asked her what brought her here, she informed me that her husband was French and just opened a hair salon downtown.

Well, that explained her great hair. I instantly felt like I should put a hat on so she wouldn't judge my bad roots. It seemed like I couldn't get a decent set of highlights done since I arrived in the country years ago. Of course, I didn't actually say that out loud to her until later in the night when I'd had a few more glasses of bubbly and felt comfortable enough to gush about her hair. She gave me the details about her husband's salon, and I had high hopes for the place now that I had seen what he did for her. Between her and Erica, I had a new level of hair envy that I didn't know was possible.

Besides the high-pitched singing into the karaoke machine, my favourite part of the night was getting to know some new friends. Katrina egged me on to tell the new-to-France girls all about what it was like giving birth in our shared adoptive country.

"No way!" I half-protested. But the problem was that Katrina knew I loved telling a good story and that it wouldn't take too much convincing because I had the bubbly as social lubrication.

Before I knew it, my new friends, Jaclyn, Erica and Beth, were glued to the story that my old friends, Katrina and Mary were encouraging me to tell. I was filling them in on the *Rééducation périnéale* I had at the midwife's office after both my girls were born. As I told them about my vagina video games, they had tears rolling down their cheeks in disbelief.

"That can't be true," Erica gasped.

"Oh, it's true," Mary confirmed. "I saw her limping around afterwards."

And just like that my level of friendship with these new girls went from virtual strangers to new best friends.

"You've got to start a blog," Beth told me after she wiped the tears from her face. "You've got way too many hilarious stories."

"No one reads blogs any more," I countered. "I'll just tell my stories to you guys whenever we've had too much to drink."

I dismissed the idea and moved on to some other outrageous story about life in France. But somewhere in the back of my mind, she had planted a seed. I just hadn't realised yet just how much it would grow.

Oversharing

I woke up the next morning less than *en forme*. My head was heavy, my mouth was dry and I felt like I wanted to sleep for about twelve more hours.

"Look at you," Kevin said, leaning on the door frame smirking. "Was it fun?"

"It was, and Jaclyn wasn't the only one making new friends. There was a couple new girls that I hadn't met before either, and they were really great." I attempted to get up and was made painfully aware of the hangover banging in my head. "Maybe a bit too much fun apparently." I held my head, and Kevin showed some sympathy, reaching for the doorknob so I could get a bit more sleep.

"There's bacon in the kitchen when you're ready," he whispered before closing the door.

"I'll follow my nose."

When I got out of bed a little while later, the bacon fixed me up and made me feel human again.

As I cured my hangover with the greasy bacon, I tested the water with Kevin.

"Last night the girls told me I should start a blog." I shifted my eyes sideways to catch a glimpse of his reaction. He seemed slightly tense but was probably guarding his reaction.

"And why would they suggest that?"

"Because I'm hilarious." I didn't attempt to hide my cheeky smile, and he seemed to relax a bit.

Kevin hates oversharing, especially online. Being as private as he is, I knew the idea of a blog was going to put a sour taste in his mouth.

I tried to sell the idea a little better while still remaining casual, because if I was honest with myself, I wasn't really sure how I felt about starting a blog. It had never crossed my mind before, but now that it had, I kind of liked it. I had an English degree, and I used to be a teacher, so I knew I could write a bit. But it had been years since I had to write a paper, and I hadn't tried to write down a story since I was in school.

"I was telling stories and the girls just thought they were funny and that they'd be good for a blog. At first I didn't think anything of it, but the more it rolled around in my mind, the more it seemed like something I might want to do."

He still didn't seem sold.

"… unless of course you think it's time for me to get pregnant again."

"A blog it is!" He answered quicker than he needed to. "Just please, don't use your real name, and don't write anything about me, and don't…"

"It'll be fine," I assured him before he could finish. But the idea of 'fine' is quite relative.

***

That afternoon I started writing for the first time in a decade. I didn't even know if I could do it, but I knew I liked telling stories, and I always did well on essays in university, so I decided to give it a try and see what happened.

"What are you going to write about?" Kevin quizzed me. He knew me well enough that he was concerned. Sometimes I overshared, and often I had a slightly warped sense of humour. I appreciated a bit of shock value in a story.

There was only one place to start, really.

My vagina video games story. It packed a punch and checked all the boxes: funny, shocking, oversharing, and slightly inappropriate. I'd never told that story to anyone without them raising their eyebrows or dropping their jaw. This was where my blog would begin.

Vagina Olympics.

I wrote the story in twenty minutes. Once I started, auto pilot took over. The story poured from my mind through my fingers and onto the keyboard. I wasn't sure if I'd be able to write, but it seemed to be a bit of a hidden talent.

When I was happy with the story I'd written, I tensely passed the laptop to Kevin.

He looked up at me in disbelief. "This?" His eyes were wide. "*This* is going to be the first story you put on the internet?"

I could see his internal struggle. He wanted to be supportive, like he usually was, but this went against every fibre of his introverted being. How could he possibly support me writing a story, for the general public, about the most intimate part of my body? I could see his wheels turning.

"You're not putting your name on this, are you?" He was trying to find himself some sort of solace.

"I won't for now," I agreed. "But you've got to know that pretty soon I'll be a famous writer and I'll have to use my name." I was being sarcastic now to try and lighten him up. "People are gonna be banging down the door. *The Huffington Post* is going to want me writing for them…"

"I'll make you a deal." He cut off my rambling. "When *The Huffington Post* wants you to start writing for them, you can start using your name."

"Deal!" I said, both of us grinning at the far-fetched idea.

If You Build It, They Will Come

It took me weeks and weeks to figure out how to build a website. It turns out, it's a lot harder than it looks. Writing was the easy part. Once I started I couldn't stop. Stories were flying through my fingers and I absolutely loved it. I was addicted to writing like French women were addicted to cigarettes. Whenever I had a spare minute, I was writing.

But the website was another story. Those easy-build sites didn't exist yet.

"Kev, pleeeeeeease help me do this," I begged as he walked in the door from work.

"We've talked about this, Lis. If I do this for you, you're going to want me to fix every problem, every glitch, every time."

He was right. That was exactly what I wanted. I just didn't want to say it out loud.

"If this is something that you want to do, I'll support you, even though we both know that it won't be easy for me. But I'm not going to do the work for you. I've already got a job, I don't need to be a part-time webmaster."

As much as I hated to admit it, he was right. He reminded me of my oldest brother, with this 'tough love'. If I was really going to make this thing fly, I would need to figure out how to drive the plane.

I spent hours Googling and watching You Tube videos on how to build a website. I went from barely being able to send an email attachment to creating a functional website, with links, share buttons and all. Many weeks later, after numerous headaches, I had finally built a website. I was officially a blogger.

"It's ready!" I announced as Kevin came into a house that had been turned upside down by the kids while I finalised finishing touches on the masterpiece I had created online. And by masterpiece I mean very basic website.

"Really," he said as more of a statement than a question. He didn't seem nearly as excited as I was.

"You don't seem happy about that?"

"I'm just a little apprehensive, that's all," he said, while looking over my shoulder at my laptop.

I called my blog, 'The World Wide Webbs', because Webb was our last name, and we were always travelling during Kevin's generous nine weeks of annual holidays.

I could see him tense up ever so slightly when he saw the name, so I jumped in before he got a chance to comment. "I didn't use my name!" I defended myself. "That title could mean many things!"

He let out an exhale, pushed down his introverted self that hates public internet sharing, and mustered up his inner supportive husband. "Let's have some wine with dinner tonight to celebrate you finishing."

He didn't have to ask me twice, but I secretly knew it was just as much to calm his nerves as it was to celebrate my site being finished.

When we had finished dinner and put the girls to bed, I took the final gulp of wine in my glass and hit publish. Then I shared it to Facebook. There was no going back now.

I just sat there on the couch, sitting cross-legged, with my laptop on my knees, nervously tapping away at the sides of the computer, not really sure what to do next.

"Come watch some TV for a bit," Kevin coaxed me. "You're going to make yourself crazy."

He was probably right. I didn't know what people would think. Would they get my humour? Would they think I was insane? Would I be the laughing stock of the Internet?

I killed a bit of time with Kevin watching TV so that I wouldn't just be sitting in front of my computer, waiting to see if something would happen. But the suspense was killing me. As soon as the show was done, I scurried across the room, grabbed my computer and brought it back over to the couch.

"Oh my God, Kevin, people are reading it!"

"That's what usually happens with things on the Internet, love. That's what you wanted, right?"

To be honest, I hadn't really thought past putting it up there. It was such a challenge to just create the blog that I didn't set up a game plan. I just sorta went for it.

The readers kept coming. I thought maybe a couple of people would read it and that would be the end of it, but it turns out that there aren't very many Vagina Olympic stories out there, and people were really getting a kick out of this crazy thing they do to postnatal women in France.

Over the course of the evening and the next day, I got all sorts of messages from friends saying that they loved it and how hilarious it was. Girlfriends living in Paris told me that random friends in the States were sending them this 'funny story' about what they do to women in France. Of course these women in France knew all too well about this procedure, so they loved it too because someone had finally given a voice to this crazy French experience that they were living firsthand.

My story was the talk of our little town.

The front door opened, and Kevin strolled in, seemingly entertained, but with a mix of some other emotion I couldn't really place. "Well, I'm officially the guy whose wife has the story about her vagina."

I burst out laughing. "That you are!"

"All the ladies loved your blog last night, and each of them told their husbands *all* about it. So I can let you imagine what the topic of conversation was at coffee this morning."

"My new blog?" I raised my shoulders and my eyebrows and did an extra big smile to try and make myself look cute and innocent.

"You got it! Go big or go home, eh, Stadnyk." I knew I wasn't in trouble if he was using my maiden name. He was being playful, so we were all good, even if my lady-parts were the talk of his office.

"But can I please ask you one thing?" He was being a bit more serious now, so I could tell he actually meant whatever he was going to say next. "It's a small town, and even though most people don't speak English, I like my job. Can we not have our last name on the title of your blog if you're going to be writing about all kinds of crazy stuff?"

"Ya, okay." He was way outside his comfort zone with this, and I appreciated him still being supportive, so I could at least give him that in return. I hadn't really had the name for long enough to get overly attached yet anyway.

A short while later, 'The World Wide Webbs' was reborn as 'Canadian Expat Mom'. New name, same author, and more outrageous stories.

Cake and Gypsies

It was the end of January and I was still trying to work off a little of the extra Christmas cushion I had acquired over the holidays. I'd been running a bit, but nothing near the distance that I was covering when I did the half marathon. Not sleeping through the night left me too tired to entertain the idea of a big training goal in the running department, so I had adjusted my expectations and was happy if I managed to get out for a few kilometres, just to keep a balance on my indulgences.

A bonus of being in a quiet country village was the long stretches of road with no interruption of traffic lights or intersections. It was easy to plan out long runs in the beautiful countryside with impressive mountain views. I had several routes, most being too long for my new endurance level, some being too short, so in true Goldilocks fashion, I finally found one that was just right.

There was a five-kilometre loop that started at my house, went behind our street, where Kev and the girls could see me off in the distance and would often wave from the backyard if they were playing outside. From there I'd carry on past the Romas, then turning the corner and make my way a few more kilometres up the road until I was back home again.

The Romas were the group of people that had taken over a plot of land on the edge of town, just a few kilometres from our house. Technically, they were gypsies. I don't even know if there's a more politically correct term to use, because they don't exist where I come from. The French say *les gens du voyage*, the travelling people, but the whole concept of people taking over land and setting up a village of camper vans to live in, was quite foreign to this foreigner.

As I passed by on my regular runs, each time I notice something new: the outdoor, communal washer and dryer, the inflatable pool on top of a trailer with a net hanging over to deter pigeons, the fire hydrant that had been tapped into and accessed from the other side of the road, being reached with an extra-long hose thrown over the power line. It was all rather fascinating to me, but not wanting to stare, I offered a quick *bonjour* to those that were setting up lawn chairs at the side of the road and continued on my way without breaking stride.

My running routine was coming along just fine until one day *les gens du voyage* decided they were going to add some dogs to the mix. In their defence, these weren't dogs that anyone other than me would be afraid of. They were of the chirpy, ankle-biting variety that some celebrities like to carry in their purses. I am not the purse-carrying dog-type. Actually, I'm generally not an animal person and being bitten by a stray dog while travelling in Central America had created a bit of a stray-dog phobia for me. Now granted, these were not stray dogs, but they definitely weren't the snuggly dogs my friends had in their living rooms that I had worked up my comfort level with.

As I approached the area, running along, the dogs spotted me and started barking loudly in my direction, and headed straight for me. I picked up my pace and hoped they'd change their mind about me. They didn't, and now they were hot on my heels. I started screaming like a certified maniac and drew the attention of the entire commune of trailers, most of whom started laughing at me.

I don't blame them. Most people wouldn't be afraid of such little dogs, but they were chasing me; they weren't called ankle-biters for nothing.

As I ran by screaming, no one actually tried to stop the dogs, but I did have a few people clearly enjoying the entertainment of watching me freak out like a crazy person, swearing in English at the top of my lungs.

This happened twice before I became too traumatised, gave up the route, and took a temporary hiatus from running. Which was a problem, because it was galette season.

Whenever this time of year rolled around, I couldn't help but imagine what life back home was looking like. Where I came from, January meant that gyms were bustling with brand new sneakers and line ups to get onto the cardio machines. Health food stores had new shoppers and memberships to weight loss programmes were at an all-time high. Everyone was trying their best to get back on track after the holidays, eat well, exercise more and trying to be the best form of themselves. New year, new you, seemed to be the motto.

That was not the case in France. January in France meant that people were eating cake. Seriously. For the entire month of January the people of France get intense about eating cake, or more correctly, *Galette des Rois*.

Each New Year, boulangeries flood the shelves with round cakes, accompanied by paper crowns that lay on top. French families consume them faithfully, because once again, they don't break tradition.

When I quizzed Coco our first year as her neighbour, she explained that the idea is to celebrate the coming of the three Kings, following the birth of Jesus. Traditionally, it's celebrated on the days surrounding Epiphany, January sixth, but like many holidays it seems to have extended itself into a month-long festivity.

But that's not the best part. Just like in the 1980s, when people would make money cakes, where you'd have to watch you didn't break a tooth when you bit into a forkful of dessert, well, the *Galette des Rois* has a similar concept. Inside each cake a *fève*, or tiny porcelain figurine, was hidden. It was absolutely necessary to watch your teeth, and wind pipe while enjoying your cake because someone in the group would be getting a surprise in their slice.

When it comes to doling out the cake, usually the youngest person in the room is chosen to randomly pass out the pieces of cake because they are deemed to be most innocent. Whoever gets the *fève* is crowned the king, or *roi* in French, getting to wear the paper crown that comes with the cake. It also means that they buy the next galette, and so continues the cycle of cake eating for the month of January.

I told Coco about the money cakes people used to make in the eighties and how they stopped being made because people were choking and breaking their teeth. She shrugged, as the French often do, and told me that it happens with the *Galette des Rois* too.

"But they just keep doing it anyway?" I asked her, already knowing the answer.

"*Mais oui, c'est une tradition!*" And that was the exact answer you'd get from any French person. This is just the way it is, because it's always been like that. Part of me shakes my head, and the other part is down right impressed with the way the French stick to tradition. No exceptions.

"Kev, this country is making me fat!" I protested as I finished my last bite of galette.

His expression let me know he was refusing to take the bait on my comment.

"Everywhere I go lately there's been *Galette des Rois* and now that I'm not running I feel like the ratio of cake intake versus exercise output is way off!"

"Tell me about it. Those things are at work every day," he said, sympathetic to my cake-eating dilemma.

"Every day?" I raised my eyebrow.

"Every. Day," he seriously confirmed.

The catch that makes this cake eating cyclical is that person crowned king not only gets to keep the *fève*, but they're also appointed to buy the next galette; and, of course, they wouldn't dare break tradition. Instead, everyone saves a little room in their bellies, because nearly every day at coffee time, there is a galette waiting to be eaten.

How the French are not a morbidly obese nation between the cheese, pastries, and the daily cake eating in January, is beyond me? But you have to hand it to them because it beats standing in the grocery store aisle obsessively reading the caloric information on the back of food packaging. Which by the way, is something I've never witnessed a French person do.

Lazy Sundays at the Market

I've always been a shopper. I even love grocery shopping and especially since having the girls. Shopping for food lets me shop without feeling like I'm frivolously spending money because we're actually going to eat the food I buy. As a result, whenever I'm feeling a little itch to shop, I usually hit the supermarket.

Sundays in France gave me a whole new avenue to peruse. It literally was, an avenue. On Sunday mornings, a nearby neighbourhood would close off the entire street and vendors would set up a pop-up market. The market was nestled between a church and a quiet residential street, with a post office at the end of the street, marking the end of the market.

With *Galette de Rois* season behind us, it was time to stock up on some fruit and vegetables and leave the practice of regular cake eating behind us until next year. Kevin was working off his cake in our home-gym in the garage, so I took the girls with me to see what kind of tasty treasures we could find at the market.

Throughout the street that the market was on, there was stall after stall of the most amazing food my gastronomy-loving eyes had ever seen. At the top of the street, there was always the chicken truck. The chicken-man had a giant rotisserie crammed with rotating chickens, dripping juice onto the roasted potatoes below, sending an aroma throughout the neighbourhood that it was time for the market. There were other rotisserie chickens further down the street, but once becoming a regular market go-er, I learned that this guy was the best. If you wanted one of his chickens, it was best to stop by, say hello (because no interaction starts without a *bonjour*) and put your name down on a list. Then proceed with shopping, and stop by for the chicken at the end of your market visit. If you were new to the system, and decided to wait until the mass at the neighbouring church let out, well, my friends, you would be sadly out of luck. Once church finished, the street was flooded with French grandparents and there wasn't a *poulet* left in sight.

"*Bonjour, madame!*" Mr Chicken greeted me in an upbeat, I-love-my-job, kinda way. "*Et bonjour les enfants.*" Of course he couldn't leave out the kids. Where would his *politesse* be?

The French loved *la politesse*, as we all should, but they take manners to a new level of seriousness. There is a strict guideline to follow when it comes to greeting people and manners that is engrained in French children from the time they can speak. You *must* greet people with a bonjour before you speak. It doesn't matter if you are in a grocery store asking where the soup was; if you don't say *bonjour* to the person you are asking, you are considered rude, and that person's facial expression will likely confirm that. The same applies for buying bread. You must say *bonjour* first, *then* you can ask for your baguette. When you enter the waiting room of a doctor's office, cross the threshold of an elevator or walk through the doors of a pharmacy, all of these qualify as places where the sing-songy style *bonjour* is necessary. Often times people will greet the entire room at once with a boisterous, "*Bonjour, monsieur, madame!*" announcing their arrival to everyone within earshot. If you choose *not* to bonjour upon your arrival, you are either a foreigner, or a jerk. After years in France, I was a jerk no more, and knew exactly when to use the unwritten formalities of the *bonjour*.

I ordered my chicken, politely requesting roasted potatoes and, of course, those amazing caramelised onions that are covered in juice drippings. This man's chickens were the things my food-dreams were made of, and I'd be lying if I said I'd never left the market early just to dig into our piping hot *poulet*.

With my name on the chicken list, we were free to do our shopping. Elodie was in the stroller and Océane was holding onto the side as we walked, not wanting to go too far with so many people milling around.

"What should we get next?" I asked my little helper.

"*Les tomate, les tomate, une euro le kilo,*" Océane shouted to me, her cuteness earning her a few smiles from neighbouring shoppers.

I was wearing my Sunday morning leggings and a hoodie, so people took one look at me and knew right away I wasn't a local. So when my daughter would burst out perfect, unaccented French, people were always pleasantly surprised, and frankly seemed quite delighted that I wasn't souring the culture any further than my choice of overly casual attire.

The "*Les tomate, les tomate, une euro le kilo*" bit, was clearly something Kevin had taught her. The men selling produce at the market stalls often called out to get your attention, in the same fashion that they sold *vin chaud* at the *Marche de Noel* in Paris. I'd heard Kevin do it at home while putting groceries away, making Océane laugh in the kitchen just as he would with me in Paris while he closed the shutters. I guess old habits die hard and he passed his quirky sense of humour down to our daughter.

"Tomato stand it is." I smiled at Océane, recognising that it was cute, yet not wanting to encourage the shouting too much or she'd be yelling about the price of tomatoes for the rest of our shopping trip.

The problem was that we couldn't make our way to the vegetables without stopping at every stall for a sample of food.

Océane has always been what the French call '*une gourmand*'. In France that refers to someone who loves good food, just like her mom. I may be biased, but with the pigtails that I often put in her hair and the cute clothes she wears as a result of my love of shopping, she's pretty darn cute. So when the market vendors see her go by, she regularly gets stopped and offered food and a little chat.

"*Coucou, ma chérie!*" The cheese lady called her over and she made a bee-line because she knew what was coming next. "*Est-ce que vous voulez goûter au fromage?*" Of course no daughter of mine was going to turn down a taste of farm-fresh goat cheese.

This region was well known for its food; goat cheese, or *fromage de chèvre,* being a specialty. World renowned foie gras and pâté also came from our neighbouring communities, and even though I couldn't get my daughter to eat a bite of spinach, she could throw back the local delicacies just as good as the next French kid.

While Océane nibbled on her cheese, savouring every last bite, I filled my wicker basket with tomatoes(as per Océane's request) endives, peppers, broccoli, artichokes, carrots, radishes, oranges and plums. My basket was a rainbow of colours, but I had to stop myself if I wanted to be able to carry my basket. I had a trick where I would hang my basket on the stroller handle, but Elodie wasn't that heavy, and at the rate I was going, any more produce and the basket would outweigh Elodie on the teeter-totter that the stroller had become.

We strolled a little further with the kids sampling the sweet *brioche* bread that was slipped into their hands as they walked by.

"*Et comment tu t'appelles?*" The next vendor asked Océane's name as we passed.

"Océane," she proudly shouted back, because when you're a toddler you always shout.

"*Quel jolie prénom!*" They told her she had a beautiful name, and the interaction took just long enough for her to spot the long table of dried fruit that was, much to her delight, right at her eye level.

"Mommy, look!" she immediately went, little hands leading the way, towards the table.

"Yum!" I agreed that it did look delicious, but grabbed her hands before she started touching all of the boxes full of dried fruit.

The table looked amazing, and I wanted to try them as much as her, so we grabbed a bag and began putting a bit from each box inside. Our bag was filling up with dried strawberries, chunks of coconut, candied oranges, dried kiwis, plump apricots, and raisins that were still the size of grapes.

"*Goûte ça,*" the vendor offered, pleased at how full our bag was quickly becoming. He passed me the largest date I had ever seen. I'd only ever had the dried-out ones in the grocery store, but this didn't even taste like the same fruit. It was plump and juicy and nearly the size of a plum. My eyes grew wide with delight, and the vendor laughed.

"*C'est bon, non?*"

As if the look on my face wasn't enough to let him know that this was the most delicious piece of fruit I'd ever eaten. I'd need another bag so I could fill it up just with dates. They were mouthwatering and I needed them in my kitchen!

By the time we had finished at the table, Océane and I had gotten quite liberal with filling our bags. It was getting close to lunch time and hunger was creeping in. Everyone knows you shouldn't shop when you're hungry. Océane had no excuse since she'd been eating her way down the street; she just liked pulling things into the bag.

I deemed the giant bag of dried fruit as acceptable since in the end, it was fruit and not chocolate. I handed our overstuffed bags to the man and waited for him to weigh them.

Just like when I was pregnant, the numbers on the man's scale didn't really mean anything to me because it was in kilos, so I had no idea what kind of price to expect.

"*Cinquante-six euros s'il vous plait, madame.*"

I stood there a bit dumbfounded. He couldn't have said *cinquante-six* because that meant fifty-six.

"*Cinquante-six euros?*" I confirmed, hoping I had my French numbers wrong.

"*Oui, c'est ça.*" He confirmed that indeed I had collected into bags, fifty-six euros worth of dried fruit. How did that happen?

"Okay, Océane, we're going to come right back for the fruit. Mommy has to go to the bank machine," I told her with a tight panicky smile. I couldn't put the fruit back now. Not only would it be embarrassing, but toddler fingers had been manhandling everything in our bags, making putting anything back no longer an option.

I flashed my stressed-out smile at the kind man and informed him politely that I just had to pop over to the bank machine to make a hefty withdrawal to pay for his dried fruit. All I was thinking was that this stuff better be good.

We walked to the end of the road, grabbed some money from the ATM and made our way back to the fruit made of gold. Maintaining my composure, although clearly flustered by the price, I paid for the dried fruit, swung by the chicken man to get our *poulet* and strapped both girls into their car seats. That was one expensive trip to the market.

As the gate opened and we pulled in the driveway, Kevin walked out of the garage, just finishing his workout.

"Did you girls have fun?" he asked, directing the question at the girls, not me since it was in French.

"*Oui, on en a acheté beaucoup!*"

Océane told him that we bought a lot, and boy, was she right.

"Mmm, what's all this dried fruit?" Kevin took note, grabbing the bag from the passenger seat and helping himself to a post-workout snack.

"It's so good!" he said as we all walked into the house.

"Enjoy it!" I told him, now popping a date into my own mouth. "When I tell you how much it cost we might not be shopping there again."

I flashed him my best 'don't be mad' smile and offered him a date to soften the blow.

The Other Side of the School Gate

All of my friends sent their kids to the International School, so part of me wanted my kids to go there for the social aspect for me. I could join the PTA, volunteer in the library, run bake sales; I could almost picture it all in my mind.

I was a teacher after all, back before this crazy adventure in France started. So when I thought about my own kids going to French school I was selfishly a little disappointed. Instead of being really involved and a social butterfly at the school gate, I was going to be the odd-mom-out.

It was hard to believe that Océane was about to start school. She wasn't even three years old for a few more months, but when in France, right.

We finally agreed that she'd be going to the local village school, and I felt comfortable with that for a few reasons: she spoke perfect French, it was small, two of Coco's daughters went there, and her little playmate, Manon, that Coco also watched from the first day that Océane went there, would be in her class; so I knew she wouldn't be alone. But as an educator I still thought it was completely insane that my daughter, not yet three, would be going to a regular school, with big kids.

To say I was nervous was an understatement.

I knew everything there was to know about elementary school. This was supposed to be where I would shine as a mom. Except we were in France, and I hadn't had the slightest clue about how this was going to go, and I didn't have the confidence in my French to go around asking. I had no allies at the school gate. Coco was the only school mom I knew, and she was at home with the kids she watched. Her kids were dropped off by their grandma, 'Madame' across the street, whom we now called 'Mammie' because as far as my kids were concerned, she had become their French grandma.

The first day of school was okay because Kevin was there too. It was a family affair for everyone, so I didn't feel that awkward.

It was after, once the school year routine started that I became the foreign-mom that the school secretary came to know well.

Canada is a very multicultural country, and all my travels had always given me a soft spot for the foreign families when I worked in schools. Sometimes it was because I had visited the family's country and I had an understanding of their culture, and other times it was just because I understood that they were struggling and I wanted to help them out. I'd go out of my way to make sure they understood what was written in their child's daily agenda and that they were aware of events happening in the school, in case they didn't understand the note that went home.

I was now one of those people. I recognised my old self in the secretary's kindness towards me, and I was the lost foreigner, trying to keep it together for the sake of my kid. I was on the other side of the fence, and it was challenging figuring it out for the first time.

The good news was that Océane was so young that she wouldn't remember how many times I dropped the ball. How was I to know that those cute little shoes with the rubber soles were considered slippers in France, not actual shoes? Nobody warned me that when your child was invited to a cowboys and Indians party (yes, they actually still have those in France) the boys are *always* cowboys and the girls are *always* Indians, no matter how cute the cowgirl costume might be. I didn't see a note saying to bring treats to school, yet everyone seemed to know it was a special day in France and my daughter was the only one who didn't have sweets to share. There was no way I could have guessed that only boys sign up for soccer and girls have to sign up for dance instead. *What was this, 1952?*

When Océane started school, there was a whole new level of *faux pas* that I took on. It felt like we made socially awkward mistakes at every turn because even though we spoke the language (Kevin obviously far better than me), we just didn't grow up in French culture. There were so many unwritten rules that we didn't know about.

I likely didn't help matters by trying to stick to my North American ways.

"She's way too young to be in school all day," I told Kevin at the end of September. "In Calgary they don't start until they're five, and even then, it's only half a day. I'm not sending her all day. She's too little."

Mama-bear was standing her ground on this one.

Since the beginning of school, I'd drop her off in the morning, and then instead of having her stay all day, I'd pick her up at lunch and bring her home. In my mind it seemed completely reasonable for a three-year-old whose mom was home during the day. But I was questioned by a French mom at school, asking me why our daughter didn't stay in the afternoon. I got flustered and couldn't muster up the French to explain our cultural differences. I just stumbled over my words, telling her that I didn't really know why I brought her home in the afternoon. *"Je ne sais pas."*

Surely I sounded dumb not knowing why I was picking up my kid half way through the day. Not only was I weird, I was also underdressed. The French moms don't mess around at drop off, or whenever leaving the house, really. You will never, ever, see anyone in jogging pants, messy hair, or a hoodie thrown on to drop off their child. Unless, of course, you were at my daughter's school gate and you happened to see me. I was the only one sporting the messy look. Back when I was working, before kids, I was always well put together. But now I had a toddler and a baby. I was treading water, and I looked like it.

By Christmas the teacher finally asked me if I was ready to let her spend the whole day at school. I have to admit that I was rather annoyed because I translated that quick enough in my head to catch that she asked if *I* was ready, not Océane.

"Well?" I said to Kevin, nearly ready to admit defeat. "Maybe we should just ask Océane if she wants to stay or not."

"Good idea." He wasn't going to cross Mama-bear.

We sat Océane down and asked her if she would like to stay at school for the whole day, and we explained that it would mean she would have to eat lunch at school, and take a nap there, in the same room as all the other kids.

"Yes! Please!" she instantly shouted. "Why wasn't I allowed to stay there before?"

I felt awful and Kev knew it. He put his arm around my shoulder and gave me a little squeeze. "It's fine," he comforted my guilt.

But I didn't feel fine. I felt really bad. Océane thought that she had done something wrong because I was picking her up every day and she didn't know why she was the only one who wasn't 'allowed' to stay.

I thought I was being a good mom by not making her leave our house for so long at such a young age, because that's not what we do in our culture, unless we don't have a choice. But I wasn't in my culture and I was once again reminded of that. I wasn't going to make her feel punished any more. I'd let her stay with her friends, starting Monday.

It Takes a Village, and I Lived in One

I had both girls with me at the grocery store after we picked Océane from school. I was attempting a Pinterest recipe because over the past couple of years having spent so much time at home with napping babies, I'd actually taught myself to cook. The produce was so fresh in France, with the seasons in the south being so long that there was no shortage of produce for creations I'd try and whip up in the kitchen.

I was on the hunt for asparagus for a tart I was making, where the little green trees would join cured ham and parmesan on a puffed pastry crust. The kids would likely turn their nose up at it because it had something green on it, but I would make it anyway because I refused to live off grilled cheese sandwiches and plain macaroni noodles.

Elodie was in the front part of the cart, as usual, and Océane in the wagon area, jumping around on the groceries. I parked the cart beside me while I searched for the most crisp asparagus I could get my hands on. I wasn't skilled at leaving the grocery store with only what was on my list, so I also filled the cart with all the other nearby produce because who knew what I might create the next day.

Océane was overly excited, and 'playing' with her younger sister, trying to put her in some sort of wrestling hold that resembled something my brothers used to do to me. Whether she was trying to play, or cuddle, Elodie clearly wasn't enjoying it.

"Nooo!" she cried for all the grocery store to hear.

"Océane, stop that please. I won't be much longer."

She stopped for about two seconds while I weighed my vegetables on the electronic scale and waited for the sticker to come out, that I then had to stick on the bag so that the cashier could scan it at the checkout. This is how produce was done in France, and no matter how many times my mom visited, she always forgot, and it always made her crazy when she got to the checkout and realised she had forgotten to weigh her produce and get the sticker.

Océane was at it again, putting forth some serious sibling rivalry towards her little sister. It was looking like she wanted to be in Elodie's spot in the cart. The poking wasn't stopping, and Elodie's protests were getting louder. Just as I was about to take the four steps back to the cart from the weigh scale, an elderly lady had intervened on my behalf.

"*Arrêter de faire ça. Ce n'est pas gentil.*" She firmly told Océane to stop doing that to her sister because it wasn't kind. Then she walked away.

She stopped immediately and was frozen like a statue in the back of the grocery cart. A stranger had just put her in her place. I was a bit shocked myself.

The woman didn't follow her discipline of my children with a gentle smile in my direction to let me know she understood the struggles of motherhood. She didn't say, 'I've been there too.' She simply put my child in her place and walked away. There was a first time for everything.

Since the half-day of school incident I had at our local village school, I started making a conscious effort to let go of some of my predisposed ideas on how kids should be raised because that's how it was done 'where I'm from'. If I was going to be raising these girls in France, I couldn't discount how the children of this country were brought up. I would try to embrace the cultural differences... even if meant that other people were 'helping me' with my parenting.

I looked around the scene of the crime at the grocery store to see if there were any innocent bystanders. There were not. If anyone witnessed this woman wagging her finger in my daughter's direction, it didn't seem to faze them. Everyone was carrying on with their shopping, and there wasn't a person in sight making sympathetic eye contact. Which left me no other option but to carry on with my shopping as well. At least now the little ladies in my grocery cart had been scared straight.

Raising my girls in France without any family nearby meant that I wasn't exposed to how people were parenting back home. I knew what my extended family did with their kids, and I remember what it was like when I was growing up; but current parenting trends only reached me through things I read online.

The Internet was telling me that there were helicopter parents, attachment parents and micro-managing ones. It was all a lot to keep straight.

Growing up in North America we had the standard rules: Don't take candy from strangers and don't talk to strangers. There was a lot of stranger danger, and from the videos passing through my online news feed with titles like, *'Watch how easily this child goes with a stranger,'* I couldn't help but think that it had only gotten worse.

But where did that leave Kevin and I who were raising our kids in rural France. Things were different here, and at times it felt like living in a time warp. I was suddenly able to relate to stories my mom would tell me about when she was growing up. The expectations were so different in France that it was a bit shocking when we'd go back home and see how things were there.

I was starting to realise that value was placed on different things when child-rearing. In France children are expected to behave like small adults: use your manners at the table, respect your parents, and apparently behave yourself in the grocery store was also on that list. You'll never see a French child at a restaurant watching an iPad; it's just not done. These 'old fashioned' values top the list of importance in France, yet, stranger danger, no one seems too worried about.

As a result of the famous French nine-week holidays, we'd travelled with the girls to many of the countries in Western Europe, and it feels like many of the North American rules don't apply there either.

Perfect strangers have often taken Océane's hand and help her climb the stairs without asking me if it's okay. They don't do it because they're trying to be creepy, but because they could see that I had my hands full with Elodie.

Another time on holiday, a man sitting beside us on a train started feeding the girls the biscuits he was eating. He wasn't trying to poison them, he just saw them staring at his cookies and simply wanted to share with the kids beside him. He didn't think it was necessary to check with me first; instead he treated them as he would his own grand-kids.

Once at the Sunday market in our neighbouring village, Océane and Elodie were both stopped by an elderly woman who began searching through her purse and giving them candy. I literally let them take candy from a stranger because how was I going to tell this sweet little French lady otherwise?

These situations wouldn't even happen at home because people generally behave differently.

Across the pond you wouldn't dare feed anything to a stranger's child because they might have an allergy or not be allowed to eat it. Nor would you touch another person's kid in fear of them taking it as being inappropriate in some way. Yet, throughout Europe you'll find people treating your children as their own. Even if it means a stranger shaking their finger, 'no, no, no' at your toddler while she's misbehaving in the grocery store.

After a little reflection on my drive home, I decided not to take offence with the incident in the produce section because it's fairly normal here. Frankly, I was happy for the help because my two little princesses weren't acting like royalty at all and they sure weren't listening to me.

People contributing to strangers' parenting in France seems to be fair game and my trip to the grocery store that day proved it. Which was fine, because sometimes it really does take a village to raise a child; and the village I lived in was clearly playing by that rule.

Are You Speaking English?

If I'd learned anything from having so many international friends, it's that just because someone speaks English doesn't always mean that you're going to understand them.

The first time Aurelie picked me when we moved to the south was a perfect example. Mary announced that the following weekend she was going to Scotland for a fortnight. I had no idea what that meant and I remember wondering if I'd ever see her again. Maybe it meant she was moving? I was so new that I was too intimidated to ask in front of everyone at the table, so it wasn't until Mary returned two weeks later that I found out what a fortnight was.

Since we were all deep in the baby-making stage of our lives, strollers were a big topic of conversations. Or at least that's what I called the object you put your baby in and then push them around. Beth from England called it a pram, while Katrina from Australia called it a buggy, Coco was French, so she called it a *pousette*, while Mary was Scottish and called it a pushchair. That's five different names for one object. Zucchini was now known as courgette, eggplant was aubergine, and cilantro was referred to as coriander. It was all a lot to take in. But once you got to know someone you usually got to know their lingo and it was okay if you used different words for things.

My favourite families to hang around with were the mixed cultures, often French and English in our community. Beth, with her beautiful hair, and Laurent, her hair-dressing husband, were a perfect example of this. She was British, he was French, and when we all had dinner together, it was a beautiful mix of French and English. You could tell the story in whichever language you felt like, and if you didn't know the word for something, you could just switch languages for a second to make sure everyone understood.

We had gotten to become quite good friends with Beth and Laurent as time marched on, and he really did save me in the hair department. I was happily back to having the highlights I had come to love in Canada, but now I had them in France.

Coco had a last-minute doctor's appointment and couldn't watch Elodie for me while I went to my hair appointment, so I quickly texted Beth to check with Laurent if it was okay that I brought Elodie with me. I'd done it before, and to be honest, with Beth now being a much-loved addition to our posse, we kinda tended to take over the salon, like how Mary was meeting me there for her appointment at the same time that morning.

She quickly texted back that of course it was okay, and that she couldn't stop by because Lola, her daughter, had her vaccinations, but that we should all meet up for lunch after at our favourite little spot.

Now that Océane was spending the whole day at school, I had the luxury of joining in on the lunch date.

Mary and I got our hair done, while Elodie crawled around on the floor between us. While we were passing time under the dryers, my mom-nose caught a whiff of a diaper that needed changing, and since I was the only one who felt the liberty of bringing their child into the salon, the diaper was mine to change.

I swooped up Elodie, made some kiss-faces and grabbed my purse, which housed a diaper, a little change mat, and package of wipes. Gone were the days of me leaving the house with an entire diaper bag containing the contents of my house. I didn't need all that, and the only time you'll see a French woman hauling around a North American-size diaper bag is if she's going away for the weekend and it would be the travel bag for her entire family. Less is more, I'd learned.

Laurent's salon was the nicest one in town. It was modern, well-decorated, and funky. I actually loved going into the bathroom because part of the decor were these cool frames with black and white pictures of the team that opened the salon. You know you have a good-looking group of people owning the joint when you're all photo frame-worthy.

"Hi Beth." I smiled at her picture on the wall as I closed the bathroom door behind us. "That's our friend, isn't it?" I said to Elodie in that unique high-pitched sing-songy voice that is reserved for moms talking to their babies.

"Oh, Elodie, you really did a doozy this time." I hadn't opened her diaper yet, but my nose was warning me what I was in for. Good thing she was so darn cute!

I found the furthest corner of the bathroom floor, far away from the toilet and the unseen foot traffic that I knew was around the sink, and I lay my change mat down. Long gone was the germaphobe whose stomach would turn at the idea of changing a sweet little baby on a public bathroom floor. It beat leaving her in a dirty diaper all day, so we'd come to expect that nowhere in France had change tables, because that's just how it was. We always managed to make do.

I got down to business, and at a rapid speed, like a diaper-changing ninja, Elodie was as good as new. I neatly folded away the dirty diaper with the skill of a mom that had lived through having two children in diapers at the same time. You learn to be quick and efficient.

The garbage can was French-sized, a tiny little *poubelle*, tucked in the corner. It would seem miniature to have in a bathroom back home, likely only being a couple of litres, but it was a perfectly acceptable size for a garbage can in France.

By the time I put the dirty diaper in the empty garbage can, it suddenly seemed half-full. They had a neatly rolled stack of hand towels to wash your hands with, so the garbage can wasn't used much. I've seen my sister-in-laws back home put their kids' diapers in these nifty little plastic bags to trap the smell before putting them in the garbage. A novel idea, but something I'd yet to see in my country of residence.

Slightly concerned about taking up all the garbage can space and the fact that it was a number two, I thought I'd mention it to Laurent who was beside my chair, working on Mary's hair.

"Just so you know, I put a dirty diaper in your garbage can."

Uncharacteristically, he blushed and made a really strange face, so I decided to explain myself. "I just wanted to let you know so it doesn't stay there until tomorrow, because it'll start to stink."

Now his eyes got wide and he looked totally embarrassed. "Okay," he said awkwardly.

I looked at Mary, wondering why he had such a weird reaction. We knew Laurent pretty well, we'd been to his house for dinner, and he had two young kids of his own; dirty diapers were not something that would normally cause such a weird reaction. After catching Mary's eye in the mirror, she gave me a little shrug and an *I have no idea* face. Laurent, on the other hand, had scurried off, making himself busy on someone else's hair.

"That was weird." I said what both of our faces were expressing.

"Indeed," Mary agreed.

When our hair was done we sent a text to the girls and said we were ready to meet them for lunch. They were downtown shopping, so Mary and I just strolled around the corner to meet them at our favourite restaurant.

We grabbed a table outside, and in no time, Erica and Jaclyn were coming from the other end of the street with a couple of shopping bags in hand, and it wasn't long before Beth also arrived, with her daughter Lola sitting comfortably on her hip.

"Nice hair, girls," they were each sure to note as they arrived, knowing we were fresh out of the salon.

"Was my husband nice to you?" Beth inquired, while getting herself and Lola set up comfortably in her chair.

"As always!" I replied cheerily, before Mary cut me off.

"Except for that one weird moment." She gave me the *you know the moment* eyes, nodding her head toward Beth, encouraging me to tell her about what happened.

"What happened?" Beth asked wearily, as any woman would when they were wondering what their husband had been up to.

"It was nothing, really." I hesitated, but she gave me pressing eyes, like girlfriends do, so I continued. "I changed a diaper in the bathroom and it took up half the garbage can once I put it in there. So I told him."

"Ya," she agreed, and was with me so far, "you didn't want it to sit there until tomorrow 'cause the whole place would stink if no one changed that little garbage can. I get that." I was relieved that she didn't seem to have any issue with the part about me telling him.

"So what was so weird about it then?" she asked.

"Well, when I told him, his face got red, and he went all awkward, not knowing what to say. Then two seconds later he went and pretended to be busy somewhere else. He just seemed really embarrassed and not sure what to say," I explained.

"That's really weird." She seemed puzzled. Then it was like a light bulb went off in her mind. "What *exactly* did you say?" she inquired with a smile. "Like, what word did you use, diaper or nappy?"

"Diaper, obviously. I'm not British," I joked.

"I bet he had no idea what you were talking about."

Once she said it, Mary and I both agreed that it was a very good possibility. Laurent's English was nearly perfect. It was the language he and Beth spoke together. He had a seriously thick French accent but he was definitely fully bilingual. The only problem was that since he had learned all his English from Beth, it meant he only knew the British terms for things, and most definitely, a hundred percent of the time, Beth called a diaper a nappy.

Our conversation steered itself in another direction and we carried on catching up over lunch.

Just as we were about to wrap things up when Beth's phone rang.

"It's Laurent," she announced. "He probably wants to know how Lola's jabs went." My now international English knew that 'jabs' meant immunisation.

She debriefed her husband on their daughter's doctor's appointment, and then just before she hung up the phone, she got this funny little smile on her face and said, "So what's the story with Lisa at the salon this morning."

There was a pause, while she was listening to what he was saying, and then she threw her head back in a roar of laughter. "That's *not* what she meant," she managed between laughter.

There was more listening, then more laughing.

"I'll stop by with Lola in a bit and fill you in. I'm just around the corner with the girls," and with that, she hung up the phone.

We were all staring at her waiting to find out what was so funny.

"He didn't know what a diaper was," she explained. "He thought you were talking about a pad. Like, as if you had your period."

"Oh my God!" I squealed, far too loud for a French restaurant. "No wonder he was so grossed out! Why would he think I would tell him *that*?"

We were all laughing now. "Well, that's what he was wondering, and then he said, 'Well, you know Lisa, she'll tell you anything'."

And our laughter got even louder, because we all knew he was right. I would tell you anything.

That Thing About French Kids and Food

We left the restaurant and went home for Elodie to have a nap. I did some writing while she was asleep, which was now our new routine.

I had really found success in my writing, and articles I wrote had been published on several different online sites. But nothing made me happier to announce to Kevin, than the day I got picked up by *The Huffington Post*.

We made the deal as a joke, that if they ever wanted me to write for them, that I could start using my real name, and there I was, now with my very own login to their site, free to submit what I wanted, using my *real* name, no longer just the woman with the French vagina story. I was Lisa Webb, an actual author.

I had a few pieces being published in anthologies, and when I first saw my name on the inside of an actual book, only then did I realise that I may have changed careers without even meaning to. It felt like more of a hobby than it did a job, so I just went with it because I was enjoying what I was doing.

The life we were living in France was such a contrast to the one we were used to back home that it seemed like everywhere I turned there was a story to be told.

When Elodie woke up from her nap, I gathered my things, and we went to pick up Océane from school. Once I said *bonjour* to the other parents at the school gate, I did what I always did and went to the outdoor bulletin board to check out the week's menu.

Since the first moment I stepped into a school in France, I was fascinated by the lunch board.

Those first few weeks when I was trying to find my way in Paris, I tried out a bit of substitute teaching while I figured out what I was going to do with the new life I found myself in.

I'll never forget how I dreaded being on lunchtime supervision because I saw that fish was on the menu that day. I had been a teacher for long enough to know that there were going to be a lot of elementary school kids plugging their noses and telling me they didn't like fish. I knew it was going to be a long supervision period. But those French kids proved me so wrong that I was left in disbelief. They were actually asking for seconds, and *I* was the only one scrunching up my nose.

It was the first time I'd witnessed first-hand the phenomenon of French kids eating whatever is put in front of them.

Fast forward to a few years later, and I had finally let Océane start going to school full days, like the rest of the three-year-olds. When I got the low-down on lunch time, I wondered how she would ever survive because unlike schools in North America, French kids are not allowed to bring a lunch from home. All kids ate whatever they were served in the canteen. Océane would starve, I was sure of it.

Each week since she started going full days, I would head over to that bulletin board outside the school and see what was for lunch. There wasn't a burger and fries, or a chicken finger to be seen on the list. The menu was often quite similar to the nice restaurants that Kevin and I ate downtown when we managed to have a date night.

While the nicely dressed French moms discussed what they'd be making for dinner that night, I stood staring at the board, trying to decipher this week's menu: *épinard moornay, rôti de dinde sauce Louisianne, poêlée brocoli-champignons, julienne de chou-fleur*. It all sounded so fancy. Was Julia Child's understudy working in the kitchen? How were they serving this to three-year-olds? Did they have a magic wand to get these kids to eat this very grown-up list of food?

Océane never came home hungry, but I was genuinely in disbelief that she was eating this food at school when I could barely get her to eat a vegetable at home.

The bell rang and Mary-Gras, one of the lunch ladies, passed me as I walked through the gate. The joys of a small school is that everyone knows everyone.

She greeted me with a warm smile. *"Bonjour, Madame Webb! Océane a mangé très bien aujourd'hui."*

Seriously? Océane ate really well today? Was she talking about another Océane, because the one I knew would not be gobbling up turkey in a cajun sauce with a side of spinach? It just couldn't be.

If I was as shocked by this cultural contrast, I knew others back home would be too. I'd supervised enough lunchtimes while working as a teacher in Canada to know that this was not how elementary school-aged children ate in North America.

With Océane now holding my hand, and Elodie propped up on my hip, I made my way toward the front office. In my best French I tried to explain my situation about how I wanted to write an article online about school canteens in France and the food that they serve.

"Est-ce qu'il y'a un problème?" she asked, concerned that I wasn't happy with how they were running their canteen.

It was the complete opposite, actually. I thought France had it right, and it was my home country that might need to reconsider the pepperoni pizza and hot dogs they were serving at lunch. I just needed to see it with my own eyes before I was able to confidently write about it.

When I explained further, she seemed happy to oblige to my request, but she wanted me to run it by the mayor first. It was a village-run school after all, so the mayor acted as a superintendent of sorts. I wasn't worried though because the mayor lived down the street from me, and had sent flowers to the house when both of the girls were born. Again, small-town living has its perks!

We walked across the street from the school to *le Mairie,* the mayor's office.

"Bonjour, Madame Webb!" He double kissed me and the girls and asked to what he owed the pleasure.

I explained my fascination with the lunchroom and asked if I could come in each day at lunch for a week to take pictures of what the kids were eating, and see with my own eyes if they were actually eating it at all. But I didn't actually mention the disbelief part to him, that's just what I wanted to find out in my research.

He had no problem with me coming in to take pictures, but if I put the kids' pictures online I'd need consent forms from the parents. Not wanting to draw further attention to myself, I assured him that Kevin had the same rule when it came to my writing, and we had a little chuckle. I'd keep my photos directed at the magic food they were serving up in there.

And with that, it was all set. The following Monday, I would be right there with Mary-Gras in the lunchroom.

When lunchtime Monday came around, I was running on Aurelie-time, ten minutes early, promptly waiting at the gate for the lunch bell to ring.

When I walked in, the table was set for the students, just like you would set a table if you were having guests for dinner. Actually, nicer than I'd set the table if I was having one of my 'casual Canadian BBQs'. There's no plastic cutlery or non-breakable plates. These three-year-olds used grown-up plates and cutlery, just like their teachers. The kids are served their meal at the table, not buffet-style. This is France, after all, where the gastronomic meal was protected as a UNESCO intangible world heritage item. There was no messing around when it came to the French and eating.

I already knew from the menu out front that each week there was an array of salads, seasonal vegetables, meats, and fish cooked in different sauces and, of course, desserts. The menu changed weekly, but the constant was that the meals were always fresh, well balanced, and, in my mind, quite 'grown up' for three-year-olds.

I greeted the lunch ladies with the standard double kiss, and they all pinched Elodie's chubby little cheeks. I was the picture of a working mom, with Elodie resting on one hip and a large camera dangling around my neck. My note pad and pen were on the counter at the side of the room, and I was planning on keeping Elodie on my hip while I took the pictures and jotted down notes because I didn't want to cause too much of a disruption by having her walking around poking at the kids' plates.

But it wasn't her that caused the disruption.

"*C'est la Maman d'Océane! C'est la Maman d'Océane!*" I had three classes of twenty-two kids announcing my presence.

I guess I wasn't going to be able to fly under the radar as much as I'd hoped. It was very unorthodox to have a *Maman* in the canteen and these kids knew it.

Mary-Gras calmed them down and shuffled the little bodies into their seats. They did lunch in two shifts. The younger kids, ages three to six, ate first while the older kids played outside. Then they re-set the tables for the older kids to come and eat while the younger kids went out and played, then had a nap in the little room off the back of their classroom which was actually outfitted with tiny beds.

All the kids ate what was served, and I saw with my own eyes that absolutely no food was brought into the canteen from home. Not a snack, a drink or a bottle of water. The kids all came in empty-handed. Mary-Gras informed me that each day at lunch there was a three-course meal, with no exceptions. The kids were to come into the lunchroom and sit politely using their manners, just like little adults, barring today, of course, because I was there causing a disruption (my words, not hers). They were always offered seconds when they were done with a course, and they weren't forced to eat something they didn't like, yet were always encouraged to try it.

Not liking something didn't happen often, though. Since they didn't have a morning snack, their appetites were usually quite good by lunch, which was evident from how they cleared their plates. However, if someone didn't like something, there wasn't a fuss made; their plate was cleared, and the next course was served.

Parents paid €2.60 for their child's three-course lunch. I was starting to think maybe I could swing by for lunch sometime, because I couldn't get anything nearly that good for €2.60 anywhere else!

I went to the side of the room and observed the menu for the week that I would be spending in the canteen.

Monday

Pamplemousse, Rôti de boeuf, Purée crécy, Yaourt bifidus vanille

Loosely and unglamorously translated by me: Grapefruit, roast beef, puree of potato and carrots, probiotic yogurt

Tuesday

Blé en salade, Cordon bleu de dinde, Salsifis sauce poulette, Cantal, Pomme

Loosely and unglamorously translated by me: Wheat/grain salad, turkey Cordon bleu, oyster plant (salsify) with white sauce, cantal cheese and apple

Wednesday

French kids only go to school for half the day on Wednesdays, so there is no school lunch.

Thursday

Taboulé, Sauté de porc aux pruneaux, Haricots verts, Emmental, Tarte aux pommes

Loosely and unglamorously translated by me: Tabbouleh, sauteed pork with prunes, green beans, Emmental cheese, apple pie

Friday

Potage, Courgettes à la niçoise, Omelette au fromage, Banane

Loosely and unglamorously translated by me: Soup, zucchini with tomatoes and olives, cheese omelette, banana

It's hard to be inconspicuous with a camera around your neck, a cute one-year-old on your hip in a room full of your kid's friends that know you are the foreign mom who speaks funny French *and* you're in the lunchroom when none of the other moms are. My being there wasn't as discreet as I'd hoped, but I did get the information I was looking for.

Mary-Gras was right. Océane was a good eater while she was at school. Kids follow the herd, and if the herd is eating fish in a mystery white sauce, they might not want to follow the first day, but it won't take too long for them to figure out that by the end of the day they were going to be hungry. So they ate. And thanks to the French and their ever persistent passion for gastronomy, they ate well, whether they were in a hospital or the school canteen. It seems to be a trend in the country, but it was one I was happy they had.

Five Minutes of Fame

By Friday at lunch, I was fully armed with what I needed to write my story on the school canteen, and by Friday after nap time, I had finished writing the story. The thing basically wrote itself because of the cultural contrast. I put it on the backend of my blog and decided I'd post it on Monday.

Kevin came home from work Monday prepared for what was about to hit him because I had been texting him most of the day.

"I'm going viral. I'm *actually* going, *for real,* viral!"

He couldn't help but smile, seeing how excited this little bit of Internet fame was making me.

"That's great, love." He kissed me, then both the girls. "I have a feeling I know what we'll be talking about for the rest of the evening," he teased.

He was right, but for good reason. Things were getting a bit crazy. I got an email asking if I would be available for a live radio interview with ABC news in Australia. Obviously, I immediately messaged Katrina, now living back at home, with when to tune in.

Another email came through from the British paper, *The Daily Mail*, which I wasn't familiar with, so I texted Mary, asking her if she'd heard of the paper.

'Is the Pope Catholic?' was her response.

I took the interview with them while Elodie was napping, and within twelve hours I had a text from Beth. *'OMG! You are on the front page of The Daily Fricken Mail! You're famous!'*

Over the next couple of days articles were being linked back to my blog from all over the world, and my story had been translated to French, Japanese, Mandarin, German-it was everywhere, and I was loving the excitement. But none of these sources were sites or papers that I was familiar with... until two emails came through from the States.

In North America they like to get their stories faster and flashier. They liked things on TV! One television network had an idea for me to host a show that went into school cafeterias comparing and contrasting the States with France. A different producer in charge of content creation for a different network wanted to talk with me about creating a reality TV show about expat moms. Both people had a video conference set up with me within hours of me replying to their emails.

Things were moving fast! The contact with the expat-mom idea had a second video interview with me because she wanted to record it and bring it back to the other producers. She had me recount some funny stories about what it was like raising my kids in France and just general differences about living in the country.

She sent me an email the next day, saying that her team loved me and they wanted to get cameras to France to do some test shooting. A pilot of sorts.

I was beside myself. I had always wanted to be on the news; it was like my secret dream job. This wasn't the news, but it was really starting to look like my little story about the French canteens was going to land me on TV.

As I skipped around the house, Kevin walked through the door. It was lunch time. He hadn't come home for lunch since I finished training for the half-marathon. He had a very strange look on his face.

"What's wrong?" I asked, concerned, suddenly losing my buzz.

"They want us to move," he told me stoically.

"Move houses... or move countries?" I cut in, but from the look on his face, I knew the answer before he told me.

"They have a job for me in Indonesia, and they want us to go when the school year is done."

"That's in two months! We can't leave in two months! We can't move from France!" I was panicky. This country that I once hated moving to had truly become home.

We sat in a long, heavy silence. Finally my voice cut through the air.

"I was offered a TV show about life in France." I reported my very exciting news in a voice that was so sad it no longer resembled good news at all. As I was saying it, I knew it couldn't happen. It was Kevin's job that brought us here and gave us this adventure in the first place. His job was the one that paid the bills and got us the visas we needed to live in the country. I had to be realistic about it. There was no way we could even entertain the idea. Maybe it could happen if we were staying longer, but with only two months, there was no way that we had time to find out.

My blog brought some public attention my way, and even though it made Kevin uncomfortable to share so openly, he supported me. He had a new job, and it was my turn to be supportive now. We hugged in the kitchen because we were both feeling the loss. Neither one of us took this to be good news.

With a sigh we broke our hug and he looked at me smiling in disbelief. "A TV show?"

Say it Ain't So

Within a few days things were already confirmed for our move to Indonesia. It all happened in a whirlwind. Boxes arrived at the house, plane tickets were being booked. Things were spinning and the feeling of not wanting to leave reminded me of when we moved from Canada.

"Kev, I can't believe we're actually moving."

"Me neither."

"Remember how much I didn't want to leave Calgary when we moved to Paris. I never in a million years thought I'd be having such a hard time leaving France."

We both smiled at the thought of how far we'd come. We left Canada as newlyweds and now, five years later, we had two kids who knew no other home than the south of France.

"I have a feeling we'll be back," he said wistfully.

"What do you mean?" I perked up.

"I don't know? We've become so attached to this country that I just have this weird feeling that somehow we'll be back."

"Maybe we should buy a house here?" The wheels were turning in my head and no matter how realistic my brain was trying to be, I couldn't shake the thought.

"Pffffttt." Kevin made the sound with his mouth that French people do without even meaning to. It was natural now. "I don't know, Lis. It would be amazing, but we're leaving in a matter of weeks. That would take financing, and paperwork – imagine the paperwork! Not to mention that we're moving to Indonesia, which is kinda far!"

He was right. Rationally, it didn't make sense. But to me, moving here in the first place was completely irrational. If we did buy a house on the edge of our move from the country, it would be an emotional decision, not necessarily a financially wise one. We should have been focusing on our upcoming adventure in Asia, but all we could think about was how we didn't want to close this chapter of our lives.

Obviously when Kevin went back to work, I ignored the boxes that were at the front door waiting to be packed, and instead chose to peruse the internet for a bit, just to see if there were any homes on the market in the area.

Three hours later I was feeling a bit discouraged. Houses were expensive in France! Anything we could afford was either a complete fixer-upper, which was not our strong suit, or miles away in the middle of nowhere, and then still, most needed some work. We couldn't do any work on a house when we wouldn't even be living on the same continent.

We were starting to realise that our dream was not going to be reality and the idea was fading away, until a few nights later when we were driving to Jaclyn and Joel's for a 'Canadian style' BBQ.

As we drove down our long country road, something caught Kevin's eye and he slowed the car down.

A vendre, the sign read.

With the car now stopped in the middle of the road, both of our heads were facing left. No one said a word. We sat staring at a giant plot of land, facing the Pyrenees Mountains, with a wooden sign stuck in the middle of the property, that read 'For Sale'.

"Do you have a pen?" Kevin asked with the promise of possibility flooding his eyes.

I passed him a pen from inside my purse, and he jotted down the phone number on the sign while I tried to contain my excitement.

The whole ride to our friends' house was a discussion about whether or not we could actually pull this off. How would we build a house in France while living in Indonesia? I'm sure people build houses from afar all the time, but Kevin wasn't 'people'. I knew he would want to be there, supervising, watching, making sure things were going just as planned. We decided that *if* we bought this piece of land we wouldn't build on it right away. We'd wait until we were done in Indonesia, save up some money and then hopefully return to France and build then. It wasn't the perfect scenario, but we both liked the idea that this ensured we'd have some sort of link to the country that now felt like home.

Kevin spent every spare minute he had the following week on the phone, not arranging our visas for Indonesia, or planning our pre-move trip to Canada in the summer, but finding out about this piece of land that had wormed its way into the heart of our family.

The price was okay, the financing would likely be approved, now he was just dealing with all of the other hoops of French bureaucracy that we'd have to jump through. He spent a lot of time speaking with our village mayor whom the paper work would have to go through. He was really pushing for us to buy the land because it was right next door to his property, and we'd become friends over the years.

"Imagine, les Canadiens juste à côté de nous." He laughed at the idea of 'the Canadians' living right next to him.

We were almost completely sold on the idea when Kevin came home more frustrated by the paper work than usual.

He sat down at the table looking slightly defeated. "There might be a glitch."

"What do you mean 'a glitch'?"

"Land around here is either deemed residential or farm land. The plot we're looking at is obviously residential. But each year there are meetings and if the land is empty, meaning, if we haven't started building, they can change the zoning of our property to farm land, which would completely change the value of the land."

"Well, maybe we'd be able to sell it if it became farm land. How much would the value change?"

"Enough to make this a really bad financial investment."

We knew building right now was absolutely not an option, and it wouldn't be a wise decision to risk leaving the land with a possibility of it being changed to farm land. We were living in the middle of what seemed like the cattle-corn capital of the world. Ironically, no humans ate corn in those parts, but there were corn fields everywhere, and we couldn't gamble our entire savings on a piece of property that might only be able to house corn, not our family. We had kids to think about now, and as much as it pained us to admit it, it wouldn't be a smart financial decision.

Accepting that brought down the morale of the house significantly.

Our dreams of being home owners in France vanished before our eyes. The only choice we had was to move forward. We were leaving the country in a matter of days, and you'd never know it if you walked into our house.

"Okay," Kevin announced before he left for work. "We've got to shake off the disappointment of not buying a house or land and get our act together. We're leaving next week! I thought you planned on selling some things last week?"

Technically, I was planning on having a big sale but I had been too busy looking for our last-minute dream home online. We had accumulated so much stuff since having the kids that the job of clearing out the house seemed too big to tackle. I didn't know what I should keep and what I should get rid of. I wasn't convinced that I was finished having kids, so I hated to get rid of all the baby things, but we had such a small allotment of space for our moving shipment that I needed to start being ruthless.

"You're right," I agreed. "I'll start getting rid of some things today."

It happened to be playgroup day, and I knew what I needed to do.

My daughters had more clothes than two little girls could possibly ever need, or wear. I loved to shop, my mom can't say no to anything on sale, and my sister-in-law always fills a suitcase of my nieces' hand-me-downs every time I went to Canada. This left us with an attic full of Rubbermaid bins of clothes, each marked accordingly: 0-3 months, 3-6 months, 6-9, etc. I knew that if I opened those bins, I'd start to get sentimental and end up getting rid of nothing. Instead I loaded up my car and drove all the clothes to playgroup.

I told the other moms that the baby clothes were fair-game to whoever wanted them and that if anything was left over to put it in one of the donation bins around town. Then I admitted that I couldn't stay and watch them go through the clothes because it would be far too emotional. And just like that, I had rid the house of every cute little baby outfit my girls had ever worn. Like I said, I had to be ruthless. I tried to remind myself that it was just material items, and if we were continuing on with this lifestyle of living abroad, it was something I'd have to get used to.

Getting rid of the baby clothes was like ripping off a bandaid. One clean swoop and it was done. It was the material things I felt most attached to, so after that, clearing everything else out of the house was pretty easy. I went around the house taking pictures, created an email, and sent it to our friends in the area, entitled: For Sale, Available Immediately.

Before I knew it, our belongings were finding new owners. Car seats, bikes, the playpen, baby walker, jolly jumper, water table, swing set, play kitchen, book shelves. Our life as I knew it was walking out of the front door. I asked that anyone collecting large children's items like the kids' table come for it either during nap time, or after seven thirty p.m. to avoid toddler meltdowns. The girls knew we were moving, but we didn't want them to have to witness other people taking their toys. That was a pain I endured on my own.

It might have been easier if I was emotionally ready to get rid of all those things, like when people clear out their baby things because their 'babies' were in grade school. But mine weren't, and I didn't actually want to get rid of all evidence of their baby-stage. It was too soon, yet, we somehow had to fit everything we were bringing to our 'new life' into three cubic metres. Basically, a space the size of the inside of our vehicle. And speaking of vehicles, we still had one that we needed to sell in the next week.

It was about five days out from our departure day that my shock turned into denial. Although our attic and garage had been cleared out of most large items, the remaining contents of the house still seemed fully intact. If a stranger walked in, they would never guess we were in the midst of moving.

I've never been great at packing for vacation in advance and packing for this move was no different. I was a last-minute girl until the end. With Kevin at work and Océane in school, Coco offered to take Elodie so I could organise the house.

My job for the week was to get us ready to step onto a plane in five days. I needed to divide our belongings into piles: take to Indonesia, sell or give away in France, bring to Canada that summer. Not feeling stimulated by the task, the writer in me decided to deal with the stress by completely ignoring the task at hand and instead, start writing a book. It was the only way I could move forward. Like therapy, but for the creative writer, I sat in front of my laptop and poured out my soul about all things France into my computer. It felt good, like the purest form of closure I could imagine. As the days flew by, and our moving day loomed ever so close, Kevin began questioning the lack of progress he was seeing each day as he arrived home from work.

With teeth clenched in fear of his reaction, I told him about the book.

"You know how I am with writing. Once I start I just can't stop. And it was so therapeutic. It was the only way I could manage my emotions." I paused a moment and relaxed a bit when I saw he wasn't really upset, then I added, "Wanna see how much I wrote or am I pushing my luck?"

After humouring me by letting me scroll through the document on my laptop, he searched for the right words. "You've made a lot of progress... just on the wrong task." Then his face turned slightly more serious, trying to let me know he meant business. "We are leaving the country in a couple days and our house looks exactly the same as it did when we moved in except for the attic and garage. This stuff has to get into boxes or get out of the house."

"It's under control," I told him. "Relax."

He was right, the house was still full and to be honest, I couldn't be bothered with the local buy and sell website online. The idea of making individual ads in French, then answering my phone and having strangers speaking French come over and pick through the belongings of our house; it wasn't how I wanted to spend my last days.

I called Coco and asked if Antoine could come over with his big truck because I had a few things I wanted to give them. Antoine built houses and he had an industrial-size van for his ladder and tools. It was larger than any other vehicle I'd seen in France and it was perfect to empty our house.

They had three daughters, who had grown into beautiful young teenagers since our time as their neighbours. They were the recipients of my entire winter wardrobe, from jackets to boots and everything in between. Antoine got the weights, and Coco, running a childcare service from her house, scored big with all the remaining toys and baby paraphernalia. But that was only the first trip. When the industrial van was emptied, I requested they bring it back, and they were outfitted with an easel, plants, mirrors, paintings, a lazy boy recliner, tools for the yard and basically every household item we'd owned. They thought it was 'too much' to accept everything we wanted to give them, but we were happy for them to have it as a 'thank you' for everything they'd done for us instead of trying to sell it on the local buy and sell website.

As for what was left in the house, it was what the French call *un bazar*. There was stuff strewn everywhere but, at this point, we were just going to have to wing it.

Perhaps in hindsight I may have relaxed a bit too much, because the day the moving company arrived was one of the most hectic, chaotic, and stressful days of all the days we've had as a family.

Our kids had been shipped off to Coco's house to play so they wouldn't feel inclined to 'help' in the special way young kids do. The scene consisted of Kevin and I, three movers, and a house that didn't resemble in the least one whose owners were about to embark on an international move.

Kevin, trying to keep his patience, asked how I planned on orchestrating this, as he couldn't see any distinct organisation in place. There were no clues as to what was going to Canada, what was going to Indonesia, and what, if anything, would stay behind in France. It was a shmozzle of me pointing at things, while directing, in French, which items were to go where. When the movers finally finished the main floor of the house, they informed me that only four more boxes would fit in our shipping container.

I was sure there must have been a mistake because they hadn't even gone upstairs where our bedrooms were yet. Stress levels and emotions were both running high.

It continued on like that until extra suitcases were purchased, more items were donated, and the last of our belongings were given away. By this point I had accepted the fact that it was all just *stuff*, after all.

Reflecting

During my time in France I was often accused by friends back home of having a pretty cushy gig. And for the most part, I couldn't disagree. There were more 'ups' than downs during those five years. But it didn't get that way without a few bumps and bruises on my ego; because trying to learn a language, create a new life, and fitting into a different culture is hard work.

But I put in the effort. I learned the language and eventually, I came to think of myself no longer as a foreigner, but an international local.

My roots became firmly planted in French soil when Océane was born. She attached me to the once foreign country in a way I never imagined possible. She was mine, and the country was hers; she linked us. Those roots grew even deeper when Elodie arrived. France is the place my girls consider home. French is their first language. And for those reasons alone, the country, that was once so different to me, in some ways now felt more like home than the one I left.

Becoming a parent opens a chapter of your life that completely changes who you were before. For me, that chapter was written in French. It's the only story I know. We do things 'the French way' with our kids because that is what's been around us since the beginning. From buying a pregnancy test to sending my child to school for the first time, and everything in between. Those were things that I've never even thought about in my 'old life' yet I've lived them in France.

And so the roots have been planted. Our family tree began growing on French soil.

Sometimes what you consider good at one point of your journey can be bad a few years later. Five years earlier, when I was unsettled in Paris, sitting alone at a restaurant, crying into my glass of wine, I was secretly looking forward to the finish line, when we'd leave this country whose language I couldn't speak.

Now, that wish I once had finally came true. But I wasn't the same woman who wished it. I was now bilingual. I knew how to use the stick-shift in our manual car, and I could whip through roundabouts like it was nobody's business. We had friends in our neighbourhood who didn't speak English, and I no longer got anxious when they invited us over for dinner. It isn't annoying any more that none of the restaurants open for dinner until nineteen hours thirty; that's just the way it is. All the things that were once 'different' about France had become normal.

So how could we leave? That was the part that was hard. That was the part that would make us stronger as a family. We went onto a new adventure and although there are many things we would miss, we would always have roots in France. This is where our babies were born. France is where our family started.

We didn't know when, and we didn't know how, but we did know that we would be back, some way or another. So we simply said, "*A bientôt la France.*"

Epilogue

Years later we did in fact find our way back to France, just as we knew we would. But that's another story, for another time.

What I do know for sure is that it was a leap to go to France, and a leap to leave. I wasn't confident in either decision at the time. The most important lesson I took away from our adventure is that sometimes, the plan isn't clear when it's presented as an opportunity. You've got to let go of the shore to cross the ocean. In our case, literally. You aren't always going to know how things will turn out. You just need to take the leap.